oUTsider

Crossing Borders.
Breaking Rules.
Gaining Pride.

OUTsider

©2014 Ruth Marimo

All rights reserved. No portion of this book may be reproduced in whole or in part, by any means whatsoever, except for passages excerpted for the purposes of review, without the prior written permission of the publisher. For information, or to order additional copies, please contact:

>Scout Publishing, LLC
>P.O. Box 31214
>Omaha, NE 68131
>scoutpublishingllc.com

Edited by Stephanie Finnegan
Designed by Erika L. Block
Photography by Melanie Rose Smith

PUBLISHER'S CATALOGING-IN-PUBLICATION DATA:

Marimo, Ruth.
OUTsider : crossing borders, breaking rules, gaining pride / Ruth Marimo. — Omaha, NE : Scout Publishing, c2014.

p. ; cm.
ISBN: 978-0-9895868-0-1

Summary: Born in Zimbabwe, Marimo shares firsthand recollections of how her status as an illegal immigrant has been used as a weapon by employers, greedy predators, and even her own husband. Complicating matters, for decades Marimo denied her true identity as a lesbian woman. "OUTsider" is a heartfelt autobiography of her journey from Africa to the US, from abused wife to an out lesbian activist, and from a life of fear to one filled with joy.—Publisher.

1. Marimo, Ruth. 2. Gay immigrants—United States—Biography. 3. Women immigrants—United States--Biography. 4. Zimbabweans—United States—Biography. 5. Victims of family violence—United States—Biography. 6. Lesbians—Biography. 7. Coming out (Sexual orientation) 8. Gay and lesbian studies. I. Title.

F675.Z5 M38 2014
920.07/82254—dc23   1404

All the events, circumstances, and people in this autobiography are real. In some instances, a name was changed to ensure the privacy of the individual.

To my biological mother and my baby sister, your lives were too short-lived. To my grandmother, you loved me unwaveringly. Thank you.

For my children, you are living proof that all those who came before you had meaning and purpose.

TABLE OF CONTENTS

Prologue   01
Secrets Are Sown and Grown

PART ONE Crossing Borders.

One   05
River Reveries

Two   09
Exploring My Small World

Three   17
A Motherless Child

Four   33
Losing My Virginity . . . Nearly Finding Myself

Five   39
London's Calling

Six   49
A Brutal Encounter

PART TWO Breaking Rules.

Seven   55
An African Girl Adrift in America

Eight   71
Death Pays a Visit, but I Can't

Nine   75
Meeting an Unpredictable Prince

Ten   83
Reasons to Tie the Knot

Eleven   85
A Temporary Encounter with Paradise

Twelve   97
The Fruits of Paradise

Thirteen 101
The Happiest Day of My Life

Fourteen 105
A Baby Works Magic

Fifteen 107
Bad Behavior Comes to Call

Sixteen 109
Lightning Strikes Twice

Seventeen 117
The Happiest Day of My Life . . . Part 2

Eighteen 119
Minor Children and Major Changes

Nineteen 123
A Black-and-White Issue

Twenty 125
Saving Others, but Not Myself

Twenty-one 127
The Past Crosses My Path

Twenty-two 131
His Ex Marks the Spot

Twenty-three 135
Inside Out

Twenty-four 141
Secrets Are Spilled

Twenty-five 147
Hollywood Gives Me a Sign

PART THREE Gaining Pride.

Twenty-six 157
Gearing Up to Say Good-bye

Twenty-seven 161
At Last, My First Time

Twenty-eight Katy Perry Has Nothing on Me	167
Twenty-nine His Fists Rain Down on Me	173
Thirty A Chilling Knock	181
Thirty-one My Birthplace Is My Crime	189
Thirty-two Hard Lessons Learned	197
Thirty-three Freed, But Am I Free?	211
Thirty-four Discovering the Real Value of Life	217
Thirty-five A Day of Reckoning Arrives	225
Thirty-six Forgetting, Forgiving, and Forming a Future	229
Thirty-seven New Horizons and Different Directions	235
Thirty-eight On a Righteous Path for My Rights	239
Thirty-nine The Battle Rages On	243
Epilogue My Heart and Courage Grow	247
Acknowledgments	249
Suggested Reading	253
About the Author	255

PROLOGUE
Secrets Are Sown and Grown

I find myself sitting on a shiny metal stool, writing on a shiny metal table, wearing an orange outfit with big black letters that say CASS COUNTY JAIL. Tears are streaming down my face and falling like raindrops onto the paper on which I'm trying to write. The cold temperature of the room infuses a chill right into the core of my weak bones. "What's my crime?" you ask. I'm an alien—illegal in this foreign land, put here in this jail cell by the person I've spent the last seven years of my life with, the person with whom I bore two beautiful children, the citizen to whom I'm still legally married, the person who nearly took my life a little over a month ago. I know not how this will end, but I will tell you how it all began.

I come from a land that many of you find to be exotic. You envision it as the animated backdrop of Disney's all-singing cartoon *The Lion King*. You imagine that it is a place where loincloth-wearing white men swing through trees, helping the friendly natives, dispensing wisdom and guidance. Or maybe you imagine it is a jungle inhabited by topless, nubile women, walking with baskets on their heads and waiting languidly for their picture to be taken by *National Geographic*. None of this is true.

I come from the continent of Africa, the country of Zimbabwe. I was raised in a family that was torn apart but tried to heal itself. I was brought up by a grandmother, and then by an aunt, who became like a mother to me.

During my childhood and teenage years, I did silly, childish things: I pulled pranks; I had crushes; I misbehaved and giggled and conducted myself just like any other ordinary girl.

Except for one thing: I wasn't ordinary. I had a secret to hide.

As I sit here in this jail cell, it occurs to me that I've spent my whole life hiding something. It is time for the secrets to end. It is time to confront the outsider, which I am.

PART one

Crossing Borders.

ONE
River Reveries

I am told that my mother, Nancy Norah Goredema, was very intelligent and undeniably bright. In 1976, she joined her older sister Lucy's family in the rural area of Mtoko in order to complete her primary-school education. This was her first time in the rural areas after having spent all her childhood in the city, in the town of Highfield in Harare, which was where she was also born.

She became best friends with her sister's oldest son, Shingirai. My mother was a wonderful addition to Lucy's family, but my mother was known to have a temper. In 1977, she was among the few students at Mtoko primary schools who had a stellar record of grades. This academic achievement earned her a spot in Goromonzi, one of Zimbabwe's most prestigious schools in terms of academics. She enrolled there for form one in 1978, but in late 1979 she had to drop out when it was discovered that she was with child.

I was the child she was carrying. My mother was sixteen years old and just shy of two years into her enrollment in high school. After giving birth to me, she left me behind in Murehwa for my grandmother to raise. She went back to school and completed high school and became a teacher. While I was in Murehwa with my grandmother, my mother lived in the city and had another child, my little sister Chido, who was three years younger than I was. At about the age of four, I moved to the city of Harare to live with my mother and her boyfriend and new child.

My mother was tall and slender, with big hair. I wish I could tell you more about her smile or about her ways; but the truth is, I have no memory to recall. In 1985, when I was five years old, Norah lay her body on the tracks and a train split her in half.

In trying to find out more about my mother's life, I found out that on the day she committed suicide in Harare, Zimbabwe, she was scheduled to move to Hwange, a small town that housed the biggest power station in the country. She was supposed to start a new life and a new job at the power station (ZESA), but no one knows what went sour or why. No one can shed light on why, after going to her boyfriend's workplace, she decided to lay her body on the railway tracks and end it all, leaving Chido and me motherless. As much as family members and friends had tried to cover it up, I knew my mother was dead and never to come back.

My earliest memories are of my grandmother Milka Murehwa. She must have stood six feet tall. When I rode on her back, it felt as if I was riding on the back of a giant. She had perfect, smooth skin, hair as thick as sheep's wool, lips so full that it was as if they had been painted on. Tucked away in our small hut made of clay, with a roof made of straw, she gave me all the comfort and peace a little girl could ever need.

My grandmother's homestead in her village was surrounded by big mountains—some bald and bare, some covered with forest. Plenty of wild fruits could be found growing in the trees. Chickens ran about in the red-soil-covered yard, with a few goats grazing not too far off. My grandmother had some cattle, too. A stream in which we bathed and my grandmother washed our clothes was a short distance from our homestead. Even though I was so young, I remember the sky in the village being so vast. At night, it was always covered in shining stars. When we sat around the big kitchen fire in the evening, my grandmother would tell me tales of the creatures of the night or balls of fire that followed her when she walked on foot to distant places through the villages. When I was overcome with fear, she would look at me and would say, "Don't be afraid, never be afraid." I've never known anyone so fearless, so brave, and so strong.

For the longest time in my childhood, only my grandmother existed in my world. I remember the walks to the nearby stream to fetch water and how I was always amazed at her balancing act when we made our way back home. She would have one big clay pot of water on her head and three or four rusty buckets in her hands. I will never know why my grandmother never mentioned my mother or father. It didn't matter, for her love was all I needed.

We didn't have much. While we bathed by the river, she would on occasion wash out my single pair of underwear, which had an elastic band she would adjust to make it fit my skinny waist. I'll never forget the time I kept itching around this elastic band and my grandmother would inspect and find nothing wrong. She would tell me to stop fussing and I insisted something was biting at me. When she finally made me take them off, she undid the stitching around the band. In there, she found the biggest lice I'd ever seen. She quickly threw it in the fire, and the underwear never bothered me again. I was never aware of what I didn't have at that time. To this day, I can still smell the fresh scent of milk right from the cow. I can still picture my red, dusty, skinny legs from the dry soil after playing all day long at the fields while my grandmother struggled to cultivate the land.

"Wheety girl," a nickname for "sweetie girl," she would lovingly call me on the many occasions when she told me the story of how I almost died as an infant. I contracted German measles when I was about four months old. Back in rural Zimbabwe in the 1980s, babies were still dying from such diseases. My grandmother's facial expression would turn to that of agony as she explained to me how my little, frail body lay almost lifeless in a tiny steel hospital bed for months on end. Each day she stood vigil at my bedside, just praying for a miracle. Then one day, I eagerly took sips of water and she knew that unlike so many, my life had been spared. She must have repeated this story to me a million times.

OUTsider

My grandmother was the first person to show me love. She would rub my chest and back with Vicks VapoRub anytime I had the slightest cough or signs of a cold. She always tried to make me smile, before I ever knew the existence of television or radio or even just other people. My grandmother kept me endlessly entertained with her storytelling; she made me giggle and laugh. I could have lived forever in her unwavering adoration of me. She showed such devotion and care toward me in my early years of life. I want to believe that her intense love in those early years is what has helped me stay strong in everything else that I have experienced in my journey. I know I was a miracle in her eyes.

My days in Murehwa were exotic, formative, and somewhat shielded, but my life quickly went beyond the riches of a rural life with my grandmother. Once I left that village, I also seemed to leave behind every comfort that came along with being there.

TWO
Exploring My Small World

From early on, my aunt Norma was also an integral part of my life. She was the youngest of my grandmother's children and came after my own mother, who would go by the names Norah or Nancy. I remember my aunt visiting us at the village: She would always have her hands full of parcels from the city, with some special treat for me. It would be something that would just make my eyes light up and make my heart ready to explode—the way American kids' faces light up with anticipation for their gifts from Santa on Christmas morning.

As much as it now hurts me when I write this, my aunt Norma was more motherly to me than my biological mother, Norah, ever was. But even in her very chaotic life, at some point Norah did send for me. I had to be about three or four years old at the time. Norah had had another child, Chido. As young as I was, the excitement of finally getting to be with my mother was heavily clouded by the sadness I felt at the thought of leaving my grandmother, the only person I had known to love and care for me. Norah, her boyfriend, and her baby were complete strangers to me.

My memory of this time in my life is very faded gray, very distorted, and filled with confusion. I remember the little briefcase for *kreshi* (the word used for "preschool" in my native language, Shona) labeled RUTH MUPARUTSA. I remember the constant arguments between my mother and her lover, and I remember never feeling at home in the one-bedroom flat located in the center of town, known as the Avenues, which was now my new home.

Then my life fast-forwards to that day in 1985, when Norah, my disgruntled mother, lay her body down on the railway tracks at Harare's train station. It was years later that I learned the true horrors of that fateful day, including the fate of Mr. Muparutsa, who I thought was my sister Chido's biological father, and my mother's boyfriend at the time of her suicide. Upon discovering Norah's remains on the tracks, he removed his sweater to cover her dismantled body, walked down to the nearest store, bought rat poison, and drank it. He would also die of starvation a few months later; his melted digestive tract was unable to tolerate any nutrition.

Even at that time, however, I knew something was terribly amiss when all of a sudden, every grown-up burst into tears and cried with such passion out of the blue. Then, with sorrowful eyes and pity written on their faces, without ever uttering a word about what was going on, they turned to look at me and at Chido.

Being wide-awake the night of the funeral, I experienced the roaring fire, the steaming deep pots of *sadza,* a staple food in most parts of Africa made from cornmeal, the tireless songs, the endless tears that everyone else cried, the feeling of knowing something was wrong, but not knowing what to do about those feelings. So like the rest of the children, I played tag and ran around while my mother was put to rest.

I can still smell the freshly cooked corn in its husks that we ate on the train ride to Hwange, where Chido and I would now live with our aunt Emma, but we wouldn't be so lucky. I'm not sure how soon after we arrived that I realized Chido would just never be the same. We were just starting to bond; I was five and she was three. Our mother had taken her own life, and we had each other. Within a very short time, Chido was gravely ill—maybe she caught something on the two-day train ride. We were all warned not to eat after her or use any of her utensils. The adults would hold her down firmly while one of them used a cloth-wrapped spoon dipped in this deep purple medicine to swab out her throat. She would be kicking and screaming; the tears would just well up in my eyes, even as they are doing now as I remember it. When they were all done, her whole mouth and lips would be colored purple. She would be so exhausted from the fighting that she would just fall into restful slumber.

There would be no more chasing me around, no more playing games together. I was five and not supposed to be affected by anything. However, I know that when my little sister, Chido, died, I truly felt so alone. I have no memory of her funeral; I've never known her grave site, even to this day. She was never really talked about. She was here; then she was gone, as if she never existed. I hope one day to be able to travel to her grave site, maybe with my children, so my own daughter can know the resting place where her aunt, whom she is named after, is buried. It is a wish I have, to be able to bring her flowers, which say, "You are not forgotten. Your life mattered."

I wish I had an image of her smiling face or a picture of the two of us together—something to say I know she was here—but I have neither, except for a space carved out in my heart just for her. As painful as it was losing my mother and my sister within such a short space of time, it was the total silence about them from everyone around me that hurt even more. They were simply never talked about. The subject was avoided at all costs, maybe to protect me somehow, maybe to wish it all away.

I was a normal and healthy child, seemingly always smiling and laughing. I didn't like to eat and was bony. When no one was around, I would just weep. I would cry so hard and so deep. I cried for my sister. I cried for my mother. I cried because of the emptiness I felt inside. I cried because I didn't know what else to do. I never, ever let anyone see me this sad. It became my secret ritual, and I believe it saved me. After I was done crying, I would be back to being a kid again, happy and free of worry, but never free of sorrow.

How wonderful it is, though, to have extended family when you have no one else. In Hwange, I became very close to my cousin Yeukai. She was four years my senior, but she was so kind to me. She was a princess in her parents' eyes. She had everything a little girl could ever desire. Yeukai and her brother, Tafirenyika, went to a very good private school, where they both excelled in sports, especially swimming. I was so envious of them. Even though Yeukai really made me feel at home, somehow grown-ups had a way of reminding me that I didn't belong.

My aunt expected me to work very hard around the house. One day, I got burned by a bubbling pot of *sadza* on the stove and started crying. She came at me very upset and said to me, "Why are you crying? You are a girl and you were made to cook *sadza*. You need to get used to it." I love my aunt, and I hold nothing against her, but those words she said to me that day are always at the back of my mind. My uncle, Yeukai's father, was and is to this day such a gentle and mild-mannered man, always kind and always has a smile.

I was so attached to Yeukai that when she would get scolded by her mother, she would get over it, but I would still be crying about her scolding hours afterward. I was so sensitive that I think they just stopped scolding or punishing her in any way, for fear it would make me too upset.

It was also in Hwange that I learned some of life's most important lessons like, "Thou shalt not steal." It had become a habit of mine to steal pieces of gum or candy (*masweets*) whenever I was asked to go to the supermarket. One day, unbeknownst to me, the guard at the store was watching my every move. I took a piece of gum and placed it in between my thighs under my dress as I neared the register. I paid for the loaf of bread in my hand. However, as I tried to scoot myself out of the store, here came the security guard, grabbing my tiny arm.

"What did you steal?"

"Nothing, nothing, I didn't steal anything!" I lied.

"Okay, part your feet then."

And as I did so, the piece of gum fell onto the floor. I was reprimanded and my aunt and uncle had to come and pick me up from the store. While the store managers waited for my relatives to arrive, they placed me in the cold room in the back, where, regrettably, tears just washed over my face. That was the last day I ever stole anything ever again.

Then there was the cruel teacher who struck me so hard on the back of my head because I could not read or write the new language of Ndebele, mostly used in that part of the country. I had only spoken Shona before moving here to Matabeleland, in Hwange. More than anything, the cruel way in which this teacher treated me because I was unable to comprehend the language of Ndebele really made me feel even more like an outsider. It made me fearful to go to school every day. I don't think I ever told anyone, but there were times I remember wishing I could just disappear and not have to be there at all. I didn't know how I could make myself fit in or how I could stop being so different from everyone around me. The experience at this school cemented my growing secret feeling of just not belonging—of being a perennial outcast and outsider.

During my childhood, because I was orphaned, I lived with all of my grandmother's children at one point or another. I was moved from relative to relative till I was about ten years of age. Some of my worst and my fondest memories are from when I started grade one and I lived with my aunt Lucy (Mrs. Chapfika) in Nyarushipe, located in the middle of nowhere, somewhere between Mutoko and Murehwa. Aunt Lucy (*Amaiguru,* meaning older aunt) was the oldest of my grandmother's children. She was married to my uncle Mr. Chapfika, who was the headmaster of Nyarushipe primary school, the school all their children and I attended. My aunt and uncle had a total of eight children at the time: Shingi, Lydia, Tawanda, Patience, Tanyaradzwa (known as "Tanya"), Zorodzai, Faith, and Beloved. Shingi was already a grown man when I arrived in Nyarushipe; he was a teacher at the school, just like my aunt. Lydia, Tawanda, and Patience were all teenagers in boarding school.

Zorodzai and I were the same age, born in the same year, and Tanya was a year older, Faith a year younger, and Beloved three years younger.

In Zimbabwe, both native names and English names are equally common. Zimbabwe was colonized by Great Britain back in the early 1800s; so dating back that far, with the introduction of Christianity and the Bible, people in my country tend to use English names quite frequently. This holds true, as well, with other countries that have a history of colonization by the British. My aunt and uncle's brood of children reflected a mix of African and English names.

I loved being a part of my aunt Lucy's big family; there was always some sort of drama. Tanya was constantly injuring himself. He once fell from a tree because he saw a snake. When he landed on the ground, his front four teeth came out under his bottom lip. He had all kinds of battle scars.

Zoro and I were very close, but we were rivals in everything we did. We competed in school; we competed at home; we were always being compared by the people all around us. There were many times I was sad when I would come home with a better report card from school and Zoro would be scolded for not getting better grades than I. We were always hurting each other somehow, always fighting about something.

One time Zoro was throwing a little axe as we walked home from school; he threw it too far and it struck me in the back of the head. The bump has never gone away. Then one night, Faith, fed up with having to share her bed with me, had drawn an invisible line, which I was not supposed to cross. When I did, she scalped my knee with a razor blade. I have never seen so much blood come out of me. This scar remains the biggest one on my body.

Then there was the bonfire she ignited, which went out of control and burned down the barn, which housed our goats. Hearing their screams, then total silence as the fire raged, destroying anything in its path, seemed like a scene out of a horror movie. We were so lucky to be unharmed.

How could I ever forget the time Tanya, Zoro, and I were warned by my aunt not to eat too much *manhuchi,* a delicacy made of fresh corn and fresh peanuts, cooked until they just melted in our mouths? We didn't listen, and, sure enough, that night (just like she had said) we all had diarrhea in our sleep. I remember the floating corn and peanuts in the big dish of water as we stomped on our blankets with our bare feet the next morning. My aunt stood over us to make sure we washed them clean.

At the Chapfika residence, we were all expected to work hard in school and at home. We had duties we had to stick to. You simply did not mess with my aunt; you did as you were told. Tanya and Zoro taught me to be strong. If I was to compete with these boys for just about everything, I really had to toughen up.

My inner loneliness disappeared during this time. As remote as this environment was, it was very busy. School filled my mind with so much that I strived to be the best. My aunt Lucy, Lydia, and Tawanda have all passed on since my departure from Zimbabwe. They died from diabetes, AIDS, and malaria, respectively, but they will forever be a part of me. They were my heroes in so many ways.

THREE
A Motherless Child

When I was ten, during a school holiday, I went to the capital city of Harare to visit my aunt Norma, who was now married and had two children, Nyasha and Tapiwa. My aunt Norma and her husband, Adam, lived in a huge house in a suburb called Milton Park. They had cars and motorcycles. They had maids and garden boys. Life here was indeed grand.

Norma was an accountant with a publishing firm, and Adam was the director of housing for parts of Harare. Here I could eat cereal in the morning with fresh milk; I could have soup as a starter with my meals; I could actually have a room and not have to share a bed. As the holidays were coming to a close, I knew I somehow had to find a way to keep living here. I mustered up some courage one day and went up to my aunt and asked her if I could stay with her, that way I could also attend a better school, like most of my cousins.

I think she may have consulted my uncle first, but soon after that, I remember her rushing to find a place for me to start school at a nearby primary school known as Blakiston. I remember the day we went to the school to fill out paperwork; I remember seeing the privileged kids with their fancy blazers and shiny shoes. As I sat there waiting, I couldn't believe that I, too, would soon be attending this school.

My aunt and uncle had a relationship that I found puzzling at the time. They would get into these heated arguments and fistfights, which included hair pulling and furniture throwing. Then, when it was over, they would grab their leather jackets and, wearing their matching tight jeans, they would ride off on his motorcycle as if nothing ever happened. This occurred often.

When I began attending grade five at Blakiston Primary, I could never bring myself to tell anyone the truth about my past, about my family. Instead, I just made everyone believe that my aunt and uncle were indeed my biological parents. It would be years before I told the truth, even to my closest friends. There will be some people, who are my dear friends, and they will know only if they happen to come across this book and read it.

As a little girl, I carried so much shame and guilt that I just couldn't say my mother died when I was five and my aunt was now taking care of me, that all my aunts had at some point taken care of me. I don't understand why I felt so much shame—why, in my mind, my mother's suicide was my fault and even my little sister's death was also my fault. I somehow thought that if anyone knew the truth, they, too, would be infected with this death curse I had come to believe I possessed.

If only I could have been honest all these years, then I would not have burdened myself with the guilt and shame of things and circumstances I could never have been responsible for. As children, we're never responsible for the actions that our parents take. If that's the case, then why did it take me more than twenty years just to be able to tell another person about the tragedy of my childhood?

I wish one grown-up in my life had simply taken the time to explain everything to me, or just took the time to tell me it wasn't my fault. I wasn't to blame for any of the bad things that had happened to members of my family. But no one did, for they assumed I wasn't affected.

In my culture, bad things are just not ever talked about; but beyond the silence, I always felt like I was treated like something was wrong with me. This is just a stigma common in most African cultures. Children who are orphaned, like I was, are really seen as "less than." They are viewed as hopeless, as having no potential, as failures in life—even before they have had a chance to grow up and do anything.

Even though we are not at all responsible for our unfortunate circumstances, our humanity goes unrecognized. We are made to feel as if we are burdensome. The same is true even in Western cultures. Children in the foster care system, here in the United States, feel this same sense of unworthiness that I felt as an orphaned African girl. Society looks at these orphaned and abandoned and neglected children in the same way I was looked at.

There was a day, back when I lived in Nyarushipe with my aunt Lucy, when a man arrived by bus. He was a tall, skinny man, with a very dark skin tone. I remember my aunt pulling me aside and telling me my father was here to see me. "Stanford Marimo," she said; then she left the kitchen, leaving me in the room alone with this stranger I had never met before. He was looking at me as if expecting an eight-year-old to know what to say.

I was overwhelmed with fear, anger, and hurt. I started to sob bitterly. Where had he been? And why had he come to see me now, with nothing at all in his hands? What kind of a parent visits his child for the first time, empty-handed? What is a child supposed to remember him by?

Years later, Aunt Norma would reveal to me that he was one of two possible fathers. He had the last name Marimo, which I wonder why I carry up to this day. The other was Muparutsa. Remember the little briefcase I carried to preschool, in the days I lived with Norah and him?

According to my cousin Shingirai, who was possibly one of the people closest to my mother when she was growing up, since they were close in age, Stanford Marimo was my biological father. Supposedly, my mother was attracted to him because he held the fastest record in Murehwa for short-distance running. Shingirai said my father even paid *lobola,* a traditional payment one makes in my culture as a gesture of marriage, to the family of the bride. So in a way, my mother and father were married in a traditional sense. They actually may have carried on some type of relationship until my mother decided to move back to Harare in search of greener pastures.

It's interesting to realize that for all the times I've cried, I've never cried for a father. I've never longed for one, never really cared for one. Maybe because they or he never longed for me.

Aunt Norma did all she could for me. She made sure I had clothes. She paid for me to go to a good school. I had a roof over my head and I had food, but she treated her own children with so much more love and compassion than she did me. Now that I am a mother of two, I can finally understand the bond that exists between a mother and a child. Now I know that it is nearly impossible to love another child as much as you love your own.

As a child, I learned to accept that there would always be a difference in the way my aunt and uncle treated their children compared to me. However, it was often my friends and my relatives who would remind me of the differences. My friend Gertrude, in particular, would always question things at our house. Granted, she wasn't aware that my "parents" were not my biological parents. She would often say things like, "How come Nyasha and Tapiwa have so many nice clothes compared to you?" or "Why do your mom and dad take Nyasha and Tapiwa everywhere, but they leave you at home?" Her questions were innocent; but when she was gone, I would find myself behind the big house, sobbing uncontrollably, not even sure why I was crying. My birthdays were acknowledged, but never celebrated, while Nyasha and Tapiwa's birthdays were always elaborate, with clowns and bounce castles and huge parties. There is something about being a child and knowing you don't matter. It hurts deep within. I would have given anything to be important and to have mattered. I yearned for my life to have been celebrated.

My aunt Lucy had sat me down once during my first days in Milton Park. She sternly told me how I was to appreciate everything I was being given by my aunt Norma and her family. She explained that it wasn't easy for my aunt Norma to have me staying there. She told me that Norma probably fought with her husband every night because I was living there and I was no relative of his. She warned me that I was never, ever to complain about anything. I was an orphan and I should never forget that. My only purpose was always to be grateful. After all, my uncle had his own relatives to worry about.

My uncle Adam's siblings, in fact, were staying at the house when I started living there. Brian was about seventeen and Angie was about fifteen at the time, and they both teased me endlessly. They happened to be lighter in complexion than I was. They pointed out that I was the darkest person there. They would tell me I needed to scrub myself really hard with a rock so I could become a little lighter.

My cousin Tanya always called me ugly. Truthfully, I don't ever remember a time anyone, besides my grandmother, had ever told me I was beautiful or desirable. Aside from the times I did really well in school, as a child I was never complimented by anyone, nor was I told "I love you" or ever hugged.

The day my aunt Lucy gave me the "Be grateful speech" was the day I started feeling guilty for having ever been born, for my circumstances, for the fact that other people would always have to burden themselves to take care of me, that I would always be a silently unwanted presence.

This is when I started to wish that I would just die, like the rest of my family had. At times, I even wished I had died, instead of Chido. In my head, I became obsessed with dying. I told my cousins that I would not live to see eighteen; I was sure of it. During most of my teenage years, I was mentally suicidal. There was never a time I attempted to harm myself in a physical way. But in my mind, I punished and hurt myself.

I was sure death would come and take me before I became an adult. I felt that worthless inside, worthless enough not to deserve to grow up and enjoy life. I experienced so many moments that continually drove home the point to me that I was an outsider. I remember the time a photographer came to the house to take portraits of my aunt's family. I was made to stand aside while the photographer captured my aunt, uncle, and their two children. Their portrait left me feeling isolated. But when I was asked to change into my best outfit of blue dungarees, a red T-shirt, and shiny red heels for my own picture, I felt unbelievable. I stood in the backyard with one hand on a hip, smiling, as I posed for my first photo ever. As often as I photograph my children today, I still find it hard to believe that no photograph of me exists before the age of ten. I'm reminded of that every time my children want to know what I looked like as a baby or a kid.

    Living in Milton Park was a lot of fun. During the school holidays, my cousins Tanya, Zoro, Faith, and Beloved would come for some weeks. My aunt Norma did not like that too much, since we would for sure destroy her house with our childish games. Tanya was sure to ruin some electronic gadget, like the microwave or the VHS player, before the school holiday was over. We would spend hours eating *mahabhurosi* (mulberries) till our hands and faces were stained purple and black.

    During these moments of mulberry eating, my purple-stained fingers and mouth would remind me of the last memories I had of my sister Chido. The medicine they scrubbed her throat with in her dying days left her lips stained purple. A part of me always wished she had lived long enough to be sitting in those huge mulberry trees with us, getting our hands and mouths stained with purple mulberries, instead. We would also get avocados as big as our heads right out of the tree, as well as the great white pears, which also grew there.

    As wonderful as 54 Harvey Brown, Milton Park, was, it was located on a very busy main road. That location led to two of our dogs being run over by cars, numerous robberies, and endless knocks on the door at night from people who had been involved in car accidents and needed a phone to call the police or their families. Eventually my aunt and uncle decided to move—only, they moved to a house next door, which was almost as big but not quite. It did not have half as many fruit trees, but it was more peaceful and somewhat safer than the last.

The white girl who became my best friend moved into our old house, along with her dad and little sister. Her name was Simcha. I'm not sure which European country they originated from, but they had found their way from Kariba, where the girls had learned to speak Shona fluently, the main native language in Zimbabwe. They had learned it from the many hours spent with the maids while their dad worked. I never knew what had happened to their mother. They never brought her up and I never asked. They just assumed my aunt and uncle were my parents, so I never felt the need to explain to them, either.

Simcha and her sister, Shanny, also attended Blakiston Primary, which was nice because they would give me rides to and from school on occasion. Most of the games we played were the normal childhood games, like jump rope. But I also have images of us all playing house in their bedroom and at times being naked under the covers. We were all girls, and I'm not sure what that meant at the time. But it may explain why at twenty-nine, after having been married to a man—a very abusive man—I found myself comfortably sharing a bed with a woman.

Close to the end of my final year of primary school, grade seven, my aunt and uncle were building a house in a low-density suburb, Mt. Pleasant. I'd never see my friends Simcha, Shanny, or Gertrude again. In Mt. Pleasant, I started attending Vainona High School. By now, I had fully adjusted to being a city girl, and my love for sports had grown tremendously. I had always been such a skinny girl, with such skinny legs, when I walked my knees almost buckled at the weight of my upper body, which was starting to rise with my ever-emerging bosom.

I can distinctly recall the day when one morning I felt a little bump over one of the buds on my chest. I had run to my grandmother, who was now living with us permanently, to ask her what she thought was wrong with me. When she told me the reality of what was happening, I was mortified. Then my period also began earlier than my aunts and most of the adult females had told me it would. According to them, if a girl was not messing around with boys, then her period should only begin after the age of sixteen. Here I was twelve years old and my period was here. Afraid of the accusations that might follow, I kept it to myself. When it came around, I used tissue paper, though it was unsanitary and gave me a foul odor. Still, it worked just as good as the cotton wool I would have been given, had I told my aunt about it.

I kept it a secret, too, for a different reason. I had never begun the ritual my grandmother had told me I needed to start doing, of pulling on my genitalia and making it larger in the hopes of one day pleasing a future husband. She had cautioned me that this was imperative to begin before my menstrual cycle started. The practice of labia extension or pulling is a cultural practice that has been around in Zimbabwe and other parts of Africa for a very long time.

Most Zimbabwean women over the age of fifty have done this or were taught to do this. It is a custom that is fading with the times and is becoming less practiced. I do not have a clear understanding of its origins or how it came to be practiced so widespread.

As the mother of a daughter and a son, I'm glad my own children do not have to grow up in this place. My sentiments have much to do with these types of societal practices and some of the things done in the name of heritage and preserving culture.

I come from a very sexist and misogynistic culture. Young girls are subjected to what amounts to child abuse in Western cultures in the name of preserving culture. Besides labia pulling, I was also taught to kneel while handing adults a dish of water to wash their hands. Only girls are expected to do this, not boys. This is something I now find completely unnecessary and would never make my own daughter do. There is a lot I did not take away with me from my upbringing. There is a lot I intend to keep away from my own children.

    I had developed an obsession with basketball, determined to play like a boy. For as long as I can remember, I had always wanted to be a boy, refusing to wear dresses and never having any interest in any of the female gender roles. Sometimes relatives from the rural areas would visit and stay for weeks before they realized I was actually a girl. My tomboyish ways made me want to let my pants hang all the time and I'd walk with a bounce. I wanted to wear my hair short, like the boys did.

    Here was the problem: I was becoming a woman. My breasts were betraying me. I would curve my shoulders inward so as to hide my boobs. I just wanted to be one of the guys. When I was about eleven, I had spent the day at the Harare Gardens Park, playing with a group of young boys. Due to my short hair and trousers, they had no idea I was a girl. I didn't make an effort to correct them. Instead, I went along, even following them into the male public restroom and watching them pee, under the pretense I didn't have to go.

    But now, how could I be one of the boys? Especially if what all the boys did was notice my chest. High-school life was so busy with afternoon activities, out-of-town basketball games, homework, crushes on older girls. . . . Sorry, I mean *boys*.

    I was really starting to be my own person. In my final year at Blakiston, in 1992, when I was twelve years old, my grade-seven teacher had cast me in a play as a narrator. That was when I discovered I actually had a voice, thus my love for public speaking, poetry, and debate was born. In public-speaking competitions, when I got on stage to compete, I wowed the crowds.

When I got to Vainona High School in 1993, my favorite subjects became history, geography, biology, science, and English literature. My first science teacher in high school, Mr. Mudarikiri, really gave me a lot of confidence. He was the first person who made me realize that I was actually an intelligent girl. I loved history and geography because both classes had the most gorgeous female teachers I had ever seen. I obsessed over both, like the rest of the boys did.

My first obvious attraction to women was when I developed secret crushes on both my geography and history teachers. I was very envious of the fact that the boys in my class could actually voice their obsessions over those two teachers, while I had to remain silent about mine. Yet, night after night, when I closed my eyes to sleep, these gorgeous women would meet me there, undressing every part of me. Most nights, I would jump out of my sleep in cold sweats, thinking I was losing my damn mind. It was too intense for me even to understand. I labeled myself "crazy" and kept it to myself.

Math was not my favorite subject, but the teacher, Miss Mediratta, a woman of Indian descent, was very affectionate with all of us. She hugged us and rubbed our arms when she spoke to us, an act of affection I was not familiar with from home. However, I knew she did it with the most respect and kindness toward us. She showed her students adoration.

My daydreams always took me places far, far away. I liked to pretend I was in the movie *Jumpin' Jack Flash,* with Whoopi Goldberg. Something drew me to her. Whoopi had a strength in movies I identified with. Maybe it was the fact that she was black and not necessarily beautiful but played main roles. I think Whoopi was my first idol.

I started to discover my passions in high school, such as my love for writing. I loved Shakespeare; I loved poetry. For the longest time, I told myself I would grow up to be a lawyer and an author. My aunt Norma always emphasized the importance of an education, stressing to me that it was the only way one could make it in this world. Sometimes she would spread out all her degree certificates on the floor for me, telling me that I could have all I wanted, if only I did well in school.

I think being a good student saved me in many ways. I always had an excellent report card at the end of each term. Being good in school was my only source of pride for a very long time. As I was growing up, it was the one thing everyone seemed to be proud of about me.

My English classes provided some of the most comical moments of my entire high-school experience. One of my English literature teachers, Mr. Padiyachi, who was a serious Indian man, just never smiled. One day, he asked someone to read a passage from the book we were discussing, without realizing that his copy was different from the ones we the students had.

As the girl started reading aloud, ". . . and he broke wind," Mr. Padiyachi irately cut her off. "Read what it says in the book!"

Again she read, ". . . and he broke wind."

"No, it says he *farted*. 'He farted'! Read what it says in the book!"

We all broke down in hysterical laughter. Our book was really different from his, and we never let him live that one down. It was a silly, juvenile enjoyment, but it bonded all of us students together to hear an adult shouting the word "fart" multiple times!

Another English teacher, Mr. Chimbizi, who was diminutive, made up for his short falls in height by being mean to us. One day, while he sat in the back of the class monitoring us as we took a test, he started swinging back and forth in his chair. He must have swung back too far, because the next thing we heard was this really loud scream. He had landed on the floor with a loud thud. Then he made the mistake of leaving the room and the entire class just died laughing, tears rolling down our cheeks. He was embarrassed and we were cruel in our taunting.

It was easy to blend in with my peers when we all could laugh. Perhaps in these moments, I felt like I belonged. I definitely felt I could camouflage better in high school. You see, I had figured out a way to hide my true self, to run away from my own truths.

Mr. Benson, the PE teacher, took the cup for broken English. The vice headmaster of our high school was also good at speaking broken English. Each time he walked on stage at our assemblies, students would start laughing before he had even begun to speak.

There was one white teacher, who had two daughters at the school. They loved horses and came to school looking like they never bathed. This only cemented our ignorant belief that white people smelled and never bathed, even though we had many other white students in the school.

Vainona was very diverse, with almost every race represented. However, it took until I was in the United States for me to know about Hispanic people. I had never seen nor heard about them in any other place I had been. I had not even read about them in books until I was in England, reading about how America could not survive without illegal immigration.

In my first year of high school, I made friends, and became best friends, with Thokozile Kamanga and Tracy Kwenda, who are still dear friends to me. Thoko was skinny like I was, but so much more beautiful. Tracy was heavier than the both of us and had the chubbiest of cheeks. As close as we were, it would take till I was well into my twenties, and years after high school, for me to tell them the truth about my childhood.

Yes, I had somehow swapped this life I had with the reality of my true self. The fantasy I had made up in my head of my aunt and uncle being my real parents had become the story I told everyone I met. However, something would always remind me that it was all just a fantasy. When we went places and people would comment about how young my mom looked to have a child my age, my aunt's unconvincing smile in response would stab at my heart like a knife.

Why couldn't she have been my mother? Why did mine have to take her own life? Why, why, why? These were the questions that would ring in my head on many nights during my teenage years. Tears poured down my face uncontrollably; the void in my chest grew bigger with each passing day. No one, though, was to ever know about this sadness I carried inside.

So when I had my first taste of beer, stealing one of my uncle's out of the fridge after everyone had gone to sleep, closing myself in the pantry and downing it without taking a breath, I had truly found my salvation. Thus began my rebellion. I would sneak cigarettes into my room and smoke them with the windows open. Suddenly I hated everyone around me. I hated my family, hated my aunt and uncle, hated the fact that I wasn't their child, and nothing I could do could ever change that. I was now a difficult child.

I met a group of American exchange students, who were attending the local university. Because they were white, my parents had no problem with me staying late at their place. It was where I was officially introduced to "pot," as they called it. I'd never heard anyone call marijuana (*mbanje*) "pot," but these Americans did. One day, I went to a school function without permission and returned home and bloodied my cousin Nyasha's nose with my fist because she said something I didn't like. I had started taking out my frustrations about everything on Nyasha and Tapiwa.

My aunt cornered me. Furious, she slapped me across the face. I shoved her and ran out, using the rock pillar in the garden to jump over the wall that enclosed the yard. I planned on escaping to my American friends' place. It was late at night and I could not see a thing. I knew they would all try to look for me, so I hid in an uncompleted mansion blocks from my house. I stayed there for at least a couple of hours in the dead of night. My adrenaline was soaring; there was not a shudder of fear.

When I finally made the four-mile journey on foot to my friends', no one was home. I couldn't just stand outside, so I went to the back of the house and broke a little window in order to let myself inside. I was relieved to enter without cutting myself up. Once inside, I slept on the sofa, only to be awakened by four white faces curiously staring down at me. They questioned me with voices laced with heavy American accents. I began crying, telling them how cruel my parents had been, how they tried to beat me to a pulp, and how I was never returning home.

Hidden away in this house, I thought for sure no one would ever find me, until on the third day the phone rang. I was asked to come to the phone, and when I said hello, I was puzzled to hear my uncle Simon's voice on the other end. How had he known where to find me? How did he even get this number? He simply said that I needed to come home so we could all talk.

I had overstayed my welcome, anyway. So, with my tail between my legs, I went back home. With my heart beating wildly, I thought of the worst-possible scenarios, like the possibility of them finding whoever my father was and making him come and take me away, because I had been so impossible. That thought alone made me rethink everything. It made me want to be better, made me appreciate so much the life I had, made me realize that I was indeed part of this family. To my pleasant surprise, when I got home, no one made an issue out of the fact that I had run away. My aunt ignored me to an extent, but was otherwise pleasant. I thought, *Could they have possibly missed me?* Of course, they had, because I had missed them, too, and life was back to normal.

I will never forget the time my aunt had brought me back a Discman from the UK with a few of the latest hip-hop albums, such as SWV's (Sisters With Voices) *It's About Time*. I was the first kid in school to have one and everyone wanted a turn to listen through my headphones. After I passed my Cambridge O-level exams, my aunt had given me some money. I went into town and got my nose pierced. When I returned home, she looked at me and just cried her eyes out. It was what I really wanted to do. After all, I was sixteen years old. I couldn't understand what was so horrific about that. Nevertheless, I took the nose ring out that very day.

I used to express myself through art, drawing and painting on the walls of my bedroom. Sometimes I would even paint with mud. I had a full head, surging hormones, and no way to release any of it. Tony, a distant cousin of mine, who lived close to us, was my best friend in those days. He and I would talk endlessly about our frustrations with life. Sadly, I never discussed my late mother or sister with him.

I always felt the need to hide aspects of who I was. I never could completely reveal myself to anyone. I had too much to hide. I would come to rely on these secretive traits many times over in the decades to come.

FOUR
Losing My Virginity . . . Nearly Finding Myself

I wanted to show my aunt that I was a good kid, so I started attending church with her at All Souls. This was where I'd meet my very first boyfriend: Lunda Wright, tall, very dark, and very handsome. He stood out so much and was a leader of some sorts in the Young Adults group there. He attended a prestigious private high school. It was at an evening function at his school that he would officially ask me out. I couldn't believe it. I had never really considered myself a beautiful girl—one that a guy like Lunda would be interested in. I was over the moon! The problem was, I wasn't allowed to go out much, which was very frustrating to my suitor.

There is one date we had that I recall pretty powerfully. It was the party we attended at a golf club. There was a dark room in which all these teenage couples sat and just smooched to no end. So here I was, with this boy, and I was about to get my first-ever make-out session. The kissing was awkward and over the top. It was sloppy and I don't know if I could say it was enjoyable, but that wasn't the icing on the cake.

As we walked home, Lunda stopped, looked at me, and said, "I want you to feel something you've never felt before."

My heart started pounding. I said, "Okay" as he proceeded to grab my hand and made me feel the front of his pants, where he had an obvious erection. I immediately pulled back my hand, somewhat horrified but giggly at the same time. It was very awkward and we walked the rest of the way in silence. That relationship didn't last long, but it was my introduction to the male species.

The highlight of my teenage years was the birth of my little cousin/ "sister" Tashinga, who was born when I was sixteen. I had to live through the embarrassment of having my aunt show up at school, pregnant as a cow, and having my friends laugh at the possibility that I was sixteen and my mom was pregnant and why had I kept that a secret. The things that make you ashamed as a teenager are sometimes the simplest of situations.

Despite the humiliating moments prior to her arrival, I adored the little girl. I changed her very first nappy when she was born. On many nights, I'd knock on my aunt's door and ask for the baby when Tashinga cried. I'd strap her to my back and pace up and down the hallway until at last she fell asleep. (At age thirteen, she would babysit my own two kids.)

After Mr. Wright, who proved not to be Mr. Right, I had two other serious boyfriends through my high-school years. Pasi was nineteen when I was fifteen, and such a poet! He would write me fifteen-page letters and was the first guy to show me romance. We kissed in the rain and he would take me out to lunch and picnics and movies. So it was on one of these film adventures, when I had snuck out of the house at night, that he tried to put his hand down my pants in the movie theater. Again, this was an awkward and frightful experience for me.

You see, I loved these boyfriends, just as long as they never attempted to do anything sexual to me. Pasi also sucked on my nipples so bad that he left one on the verge of falling off! I stayed with him for a long time, after he agreed not to push the issue of having sex. That promise helped a lot, but after a while I just got plain bored. I dated guys because that was all I knew to be possible. When I slept at night, however, it was girls I dreamt about.

Belinda, in particular, was a girl four years my senior. Even though I could not understand this thing that just made me want her attention so much, I followed her on the athletic fields like a little lost puppy dog. I would offer to hold her shoes while she ran, because she was one of the best sprinters in the entire school. When she came back for her shoes, I would ask her to hug me before I would give the shoes back. She thought

I was cute. . . . Little did she or I know, but I was really in love.

By the time I was in lower six, after passing my O levels at seventeen, a heartthrob from a different school was now at my high school. His name was Masimba. He was ever so tall, light complexioned, dazzling smile, good basketball player. Name it and this guy had it. There was only one problem: Every girl in school saw what I saw. So, in retrospect, I stood no chance. I never attempted to attract him, but it was he who pursued me, instead. Much to my delight, of course! I think this was the first time I was truly in love with someone.

One day, I intentionally left way early from school, borrowed my best friend Thoko's bike, and rode out of town to Masimba's house while his parents worked. He had invited his other friend, who had brought a girl with him. We had drunk his father's expensive liquor and were all wasted. The friend took the girl to Masimba's bedroom and locked the door. Masimba motioned me to come to the door, where he had a chair. Standing on it, looking through the glass above the door, for the first time in my life, I witnessed two people having sex right before my eyes. Of course, I had seen sex in the pornos my uncle kept in a locked suitcase in his wardrobe. They were all very disgusting, but somewhat addictive to the eyes of a seventeen-year-old virgin.

This was a crazy thing to watch in real life. First of all, I couldn't believe that this girl of my age was having full-blown sex with a boy. Another part of my mind was wondering, *What is Masimba thinking?* In our drunken laughter, the chair fell over, bringing the grinding inside the bedroom to a halt. The two came out and we replaced them in his bedroom. We had sex, but I was too drunk to remember the actual details of the act itself. I know he had at least taken the time to put on a condom.

I have no recollection of any emotions attached to this experience. I know we heard the gate open outside and were horrified to learn real quickly that his father was home much earlier than we had expected. I quickly threw my school uniform back on and rushed next door to his half sister Tendai's room. Tendai was the same age as we were and also attended Vainona. At this very moment, she was probably studiously doing her work in class, with no idea of the drama that was unfolding at her house. Once in her room, I hid in her wardrobe. Meanwhile, Masimba went out to greet his father and made some excuse about being sick, which was why he was home from school. These grown-ups, I tell you, were so gullible! Could Masimba's father not tell by the stench on his breath or the redness in his eye that his son was blatantly lying to him?

The next thing I heard was Masimba whispering outside Tendai's bedroom window for me to come out and escape while his father fixed something in the kitchen to eat. In my head, I was screaming, *Are you out of your mind? If I'm caught, I'm dead meat.*

"Well," Masimba said, "if you want to get out of there, it's now or never."

I took a deep breath, said a little prayer, and slowly stepped out on my tiptoes. In the hallway, I could see the back of this man's head, with one 90-degree turn he would surely catch me and my life as I knew it would be over. Somehow I escaped out the door, without being noticed. I hurried out the gate and Masimba was waiting out there, holding on to Thoko's bike. The other two must have run off while we were occupied in Masimba's bedroom.

As I rode back to school and the wind helped me sober up, I could not believe what just transpired. My first thoughts were *I'm pregnant* and *How, on God's green earth, could I ever be so stupid?*

I'm riddled with shame and guilt. *With everything I've gone through, this is what I've chosen for myself: to be a pregnant teenager. What a shame! What if I had gotten caught by his father? What, then? What about school? Did anyone notice me enter, then leave before the day was over?*

It was then I vowed not to ever have sex again until I was married to someone, lest I forget I was a product of unprotected teenage sex, and I'd never want to repeat it. Honestly, I could not fathom why sex was supposedly so great, anyway. I had done it and no fireworks had exploded. The sky hadn't parted. Instead, all I had were these intense feelings of shame. Luckily, days went by, and before the month was over my worst enemy, Mother Nature, came around. I bled and, for the first time in my teenage life, was happy to menstruate.

Masimba and I carried on with this thing. We were more like best friends; sex was not the primary part of it. There was no intercourse, but he taught me things about my body, about the power of touch. In our final year of high school, we would sit for hours in the school library. When no one was around, he would slip a hand inside my school skirt, underneath the table, and just touch and circle with his fingers. He brought about such intense feelings of pleasure in me. As long as it didn't go any further, I was okay. He would be the first man I would attempt to put my mouth on. It was somewhat nauseating to me, but pleasurable at least for him.

During this time, how could I not have known my truth? At night, dreams of my beautiful female teachers constantly invaded my sleep. What about the much older girls throughout the years whom I had so secretly admired? Not only Belinda, but also Paris and Charity. How could they not tell how much I wanted their attention? I would do anything to be around them. How could I not see for myself the person that I was?

These inklings of awareness came, and then quickly went away. On the surface, I was now a typical eighteen-year-old girl. High school was over.

FIVE
London's Calling

Two days after taking my final A-level exam, I was on a plane to England with my aunt and little sister Tashinga in tow. I was going to work as a maid for a Zimbabwean doctor and his wife. Yes, it was terribly sad that I would be someone's maid. But, like my aunt had said, "Ruth, this is only a stepping-stone." There was no reason to remain in Zimbabwe. The economy was already starting a downward tumble, and this would be best if I wanted a better life.

Masimba had cried inconsolably at the airport the night I left. I had vowed to always be true, vowed that he was my only true love and that someday soon we would be together again. Boy, was I wrong!

We arrived in Surrey, England, in January 1998, and we stayed at a distant aunt's house. Tina was her name, and she was hospitable. In two days, she would drive me and my aunt to meet this new family for whom I would be a maid. I knew I was very hardworking; my aunt had made sure I did all my own laundry from the time I started staying with her, even though the family maid had done everyone else's. On Sundays, when the maid was off, I was the one who cleaned the house, so I was very familiar with housework. I knew the Zimbabwean doctor and his wife had a two-year-old and another one on the way, which was why they so desperately needed a young girl from home to help them out. Honestly, who in England would stay and be a maid and get paid one hundred pounds a month? (In American terms, that was about $163 a month.)

During the entire ride to this house, my heart felt heavy. I kept thinking that no matter how much of a better life my aunt would have wanted for, let's say Nyasha, her own biological child, would she ever really make her daughter be a maid for someone in the hope she would make something out of it? The answer came back as no. Once again, I was reminded that I was an outcast. I was an orphan. No matter how much I denied it, it would always be true. I tried my best to hold back the tears, which were pushing against my eyelids.

When we arrived, the couple was very pleasant. They showed my aunts the room I'd stay in. Their little girl hit it off with Tashinga, who was now almost three. I connected with their child as well, maybe because I could see Tashinga in her. My new masters discussed all the details with my aunts; then it was time for them to go. I would be left in this house, in this country that was so far and distant from home. As they hugged me good-bye, I could no longer hold back the tears. I was overwhelmed by the thought of not seeing Tashinga again, not seeing my grandmother every day, like I had done since I was ten, the thought of all my cousins left back home, all my friends—all at once, I felt like the little girl of five whom people had stared at with pity in their eyes as they buried her mother, who had taken her own life. I felt helpless and I felt alone.

Tashinga cried as well, calling my name and raising her arms in protest for me to hold her. My aunt Norma showed little emotion, and acted surprised that I was reacting in this manner. Was it a defense mechanism for her, or did she really think this was what was best for me? Without further ado, they left and I quickly had to come to terms with my new reality. I had to gather myself together. With haste, the lady of the house went into showing me where everything went and telling me in detail her little girl's schedule. I fell asleep that night with so much anger, sadness, and sorrow. But guess who was back the very next day to get me? Yes, my aunts. I guess somehow Tina had convinced Aunt Norma that there had to be a better way for me to start out my life in England, and Tina had agreed to let me stay at her place and help me get into school. Just like that, I left the doctor's house, never to return.

My aunt and baby sister would return home to Zimbabwe shortly after. Once again, the good-bye at the airport would be gut-wrenching for me. We had managed to celebrate my nineteenth birthday, complete with a cake, on January 17, just before they left. That was terrific. So I stayed at this flat in Reigate, Surrey, with this aunt I had never met or spoken to before my arrival in England. She had two sons—Simba, about fourteen, and Tanaka, about ten.

Residing with her was another woman from Zimbabwe, who was somewhat of a chronic liar. She told me repeatedly of her son she had left back home. I would come to find out that she had a little girl back home, not a little boy. For the longest time, I was so confused as to why someone would lie about something like that. Then I remembered the shame and stigma that affects most Third World countries and cultures when it comes to gender. Most people would much rather have boys. For many years, I myself had thought that if I had been born a boy, my father—whichever one it was—would have wanted me and would have somehow pursued a relationship with me.

Also staying in this two-bedroom flat was a distant cousin, Christopher, who would become a friend, confidant, and something else. Christopher got a job polishing furniture at a furniture store that was closing. On a day that he needed extra help, and Simba was unable to go, I went and made a hundred pounds a day, literally making a fortune at the very first job that I ever held. The night before this, I had dreamt I was fishing in a river and the fish were literally jumping into my net all by themselves. My grandmother had always told me that if I dreamt of fish, then money would be coming my way. I had never believed it.

It was strange, but literally just days before, I was supposed to be a maid and making that much in a whole month. The days were long, hard, and bitterly cold. We would start off staining wood chairs and tables in oak, let them dry out, then polish them with wax for hours on end. Our days would start at six in the morning and would end sometimes past midnight. The guy who owned the shop was a fat, bald Englishman who, after his divorce, had met a skinny girl from Thailand. He was now moving there to get away from his ex-wife. At the end of the week, I couldn't believe how much money I had made—more money than I had seen in my entire life. I soon opened a bank account and sent some money to my aunt back home in Zimbabwe. As strong as the pound was compared to the Zimbabwean dollar, the money I sent back would be in the thousands. I was proud of myself, feeling like I was finally giving back to the people who had given so much to me for so long.

On long days at the furniture shop, I would reminisce about the vacations we took to the mighty Victoria Falls and the Great Kariba with my family and my aunt Ann and uncle Simon, who were among my favorites.

Oddly, Tina, who had been so welcoming, was now rather bitter toward me, demanding I help out with bills, which I obliged. But then came the rumors to my aunt back home that I was partying all the time, and that I didn't help out enough. The list of complaints was endless. One night we got into a big argument and I walked across town, through a deserted park and graveyard. It was way past midnight when I arrived at the only public telephone booth I knew of. I called my aunt Norma and cried that I just wanted to come home. Instead, I was told to apologize and work things out, so I did.

Some emergency came up with Christopher's family back in Zimbabwe and he had to return home. This was a relief because our relationship was crossing the lines of being related. We had made out on drunken nights and we spent way too much time together with the furniture job. (I thank God to this day that it never went further.) While in England, I was still in communication with my high-school boyfriend Masimba, who was now working for a bank back in Zimbabwe. Of course, I now knew it wouldn't be forever, but would I ever tell him that? Absolutely not. My best friend, Thoko, had written and confessed to me that she was pregnant by her longtime boyfriend, Farai, but she had not told her family, who were sure to disown her. I'd sent money to Masimba, and may have sent Thoko some, too. It felt good to be in this position to be able to have money.

After a few months in England, I got in contact with my aunt Algar, my cousin Octavia's mother. We arranged to meet at Gatwick Airport when Octavia was returning home from a trip; then I would go and visit with them in Birmingham. My aunt Algar, just like my aunt Ann, was one of my mother's many half brothers and sisters. My maternal grandfather had many wives in the time he was alive. I never got to meet the man.

On May 2, 1978, my grandfather Kenneth Victor Goredema was shot in the head when he answered a knock in the middle of the night in his home during the Chimurenga War. It might have been a group of the guerillas known as *macomrades,* or it could have been the soldiers. During this time of war in my country, if a prominent businessman, like my grandfather, had shown any support for either side, then he was sure to be an enemy to the opposite group. His file still exists in Chinhoyi, Zimbabwe; the case was never solved. These same people, I'm told, captured my biological mother, Norah, and kept her for a period of time. They were known to torture and rape the women they captured.

The Chimurenga War was a period of unrest in Zimbabwe and civilians were subjected to curfews and wrongful persecution and execution. At some point before my grandfather's death, my grandmother decided to leave him after discovering that he was having an affair with a much younger woman. My grandmother was herself married three different times and had a total of six children: Lucy, Emma, John, Norah, Norma, and the one to make six died in infancy. Only Norma and Norah were my grandfather Kenneth Victor Goredema's children—the rest of my biological mother's siblings had different fathers.

This idea of visiting my relatives in Birmingham was delightful. I had last seen my cousin Octavia when she had first visited Zimbabwe at age fifteen and I was fourteen. Octavia had changed the way I looked at the world at that time. I remember her scolding me for being interested in wrestling, telling me that in England only ten-year-old boys, like her little brother, Farai, watched wrestling. So from then on, I no longer liked it. At a party we had at my house, she had shown interest in this older boy. I couldn't believe her boldness as she was not scared to approach him. Her Western influence had been tremendous to me back then, even the way I dressed was different after her visit.

Though it had only been about five years since I last saw her, it felt like it had been a lifetime. I longed so much to form a bond with this long-lost cousin from this different world. It seemed to me like her life was years ahead of mine. She already had her own car and her own life, essentially; I had great admiration for her. My first night at their house in Birmingham, we stayed up late and she told me stories about how she was involved in a car accident, which was her fault, and had not disclosed to her mom that she was not wearing any shoes while she drove. She told me how she had cheated on a boyfriend, who then ended the relationship upon discovering this. She was trusting me with these secrets, which, of course, I am now disclosing, but only because she has done so much since that time!

I only stayed a few days, which were filled with Octavia showing me her town and taking me to places. I took the train back to Surrey with my music blasting through my ears from my Discman. My camouflage cargo pants were baggy against my frame and my Nike hat was pulled tight—only sparse, short, and spiky dreadlocks escaped through the sides of my cap. I had always been a tomboy and dressed more boyish than feminine for as long as I could remember. Even as a little girl growing up in a society where gender roles were so black and white, I had always insisted on wearing pants instead of dresses. I always preferred my hair short than long. I had always felt more comfortable dressing like a boy than as a girl.

I was back in Reigate, where once again the gloomy weather and cold drizzles of England affected my every sense of being. The furniture shop soon closed, and I had to look for alternative work, having entered as a visitor and nothing more. I couldn't legally work, but my aunt somehow got me a job at some retirement home. Its name I don't care to remember. With no training whatsoever, I was thrust into this place that housed old, old English people. I had to wear one of my aunt's oversized nursing dresses, made to fit her size-twenty frame as opposed to my size four. I had to wear one of her wigs, as I had to cover up my budding dreadlocks. This was simply not me. Then it happened on that very first day on the job, I was asked by the person I was working with to empty a commode full of poop. Oh, my God! The smell was enough to create an atomic bomb. Then gloveless, I had to spray this container clean. I swallowed hard, forcing the immense nauseating feeling back into my stomach. I went three straight days without eating after this, but I stayed at the job.

While walking home one day, I came across a tattoo shop, where I would get my first tattoo. I got a rose, on the right side of my belly, just below my navel. I had walked into the shop with no idea of what I was getting. I knew where I wanted to get it, though. I had a little scar there from when the "Prophet" (*Muporofita*) had come to our house when I was sixteen.

I truly can't remember the exact reason why the Prophet had been summoned to our house in the first place. However, I know it had nothing to do with me. He just happened to end up diagnosing me while he was there. He had taken one look at me and had prophesized that "they" had put a curse on me. He had summoned my grandmother and my aunt to hold me down while he extracted the thing they had planted in me. I lay there on the ground of our tiled kitchen floor, with my belly exposed. He took his hand and dipped it in the basin of water next to me, then in some salt on a saucer. With all the force in his body, he dug his fingers and nails against my flesh while chanting in a foreign tongue. I looked down in pain and could see the bloody track his fingers left behind as he pulled this thing out of my midsection. To this day, I don't know how it was possible; but, like magic, when he was done, he had this weirdly shaped bone, which was wrapped in red and black beads. It pulsed as if it had a beating heart. He held it in his hand for us all to see, urging us to feel it.

No, this was not happening in some scary movie. It had just happened on my kitchen floor. The thing was buried somewhere in my backyard, which was, of course, never the same to me. From then on, I would avoid this part of the yard, fearing its escape from the ground and back into my body. African juju really existed, no matter how much I didn't believe in it. I had seen with my own eyes a breathing bone with beads extracted out of me. To this day, I'm baffled by this. It was never talked about, and I will never know who "they" were. The scar was the last reminder of that experience, and I decided I would cover that part of my body with a rose tattoo. I would never revisit that day in my mind, until now as I am telling you about it.

I soon began looking for enrollment at universities. Luckily at the time, a Zimbabwean could easily transform a visitor's visa into a student one without having to return home, since Zimbabwe was a British colony. At one of the universities in London, I would meet a girl with whom I went to Vainona. Tinazvo was excited to see someone from school, so we exchanged contact information. It turned out to be a blessing, as I would get kicked out by my aunt after a huge fight. I found myself dialing Tinazvo to see if I could go and stay with her, wherever she lived. The thought of contacting Aunt Algar in Birmingham crossed my mind, but I decided that relatives would not be a good idea. Instead, I was off to central London, dragging my belongings in a huge suitcase to live with a girl I barely talked to in school.

On arrival, I immediately felt unwelcome. Tinazvo had other roommates, who did not hide their disapproval of an unexpected addition to the small flat. She was kind, though, sharing the little space she had with me. I soon became a nuisance; my extreme drinking became the talk of the house. In my mind, I simply enjoyed the Strongbow hard apple cider and didn't see a problem with having one throughout the day. The little money I had saved up was running out; I no longer had a job; I was not yet enrolled in school; my six-month allowance of entry was close to expiration.

I called home, pleading for some type of help or maybe for the permission to just return home. Clearly, life in England was not turning out so great. Not to worry, my aunt Norma said, her business associate would be in Oxford soon and she would ask him to leave me a few hundred pounds. With that money, I should buy a ticket to America, since my aunt had made sure to secure a visa for me before I left Zimbabwe.

Interestingly, I had applied for nursing school just the week before. The interview had seemed promising, so I was not sure this was a good time to leave England. In the nursing program, they would pay me a bursary, or scholarship, to attend school, as well as give me accommodation. They would also give me a student visa, which would allow me to remain in the country legally.

SIX
A Brutal Encounter

As soon as I got word that my aunt's business associate was in Oxford, I took the train there, not sure what to expect. I'd find out real quick. I got to the hotel where he was staying and, after inquiring about his room, I was shown the way there. I waited at the door and knocked—suddenly aware that I was standing at the door of a strange man. My aunt had worked at this publishing company a long time, and I had gone to her job on many occasions growing up. I, however, had never in all that time met this particular business associate who was now on the other side of this door, and to whom I would soon be acquainted. I got a slight sinking in my stomach, but I ignored it, saying to myself how silly it was to be fearful. *He is my mother's boss, for Christ's sake. He wouldn't do anything to me.*

A hoarse voice responded by telling me to come in. I opened the door slowly, and there were two men in the room. The one I first noticed was the very stout man sitting in the corner, spilling out of his chair. He had a big smile on his face and his arms were stretched out.

"Come over here," he said. "I've been waiting for you."

As I got close, maybe to give him a hug, even though I'm not sure why I would be hugging a total stranger, he reached out and grabbed both my breasts. He squeezed, as if this was just a normal cultural greeting or something. I pulled back, repulsed. I retreated, thinking I should bolt out the door. My reaction surprised him.

"What's wrong?" he said.

What's wrong? I thought. "Why would you do that?" I found myself responding aloud.

"Oh . . ." He laughed. "It's what I do. Don't be scared, even your mom knew when she sent you to me that I would do this. Now just come over here."

The other man looked and said nothing; tears started to roll down my face. I once again got the image of a little girl, maybe four or five, lying in a maize field. A fat man, exposed, was on top of her, trying to force himself on her, but he fails. Had this happened to me? I didn't know if it was just a figment of my imagination, but I knew it was an image that would cross my thoughts in unpleasant situations, like the one I was now faced with.

I somehow got the strength to calm myself down, suddenly remembering how much I needed this man's money. I sat on the bed and talked to these men, acting as if all was fine in the world. I was told I would return the following day after he gave me the five hundred pounds my mother had asked him to give me. Certainly, he would make sure I had my own room for the night. Soon the other man would leave and I would be left alone in this dark hotel room with this man, who could have easily weighed a ton.

That night, I let my body become numb as he violated me, touching my breasts, while telling me about all the girls who had let him do this to them. One of them, he told me, was my favorite cousin. I couldn't believe what I was hearing, not my dear cousin. I knew she was working for one of his new companies. To me, this was more shocking than anything else that followed. He removed his pants and, due to his sagging stomach, his penis was not visible to my eyes. I found myself letting out a loud scream as he tried to mount himself on top of me. He grabbed my mouth with both of his hands to shut me up. I told him if he tried to rape me, I would scream. I told him there was no way I would allow him to violate me in that way. I told him I would rather be homeless on the street than be raped for money.

I must have convinced him. He told me to go to the room he had paid for and to come back and collect the money in the morning. That night, using the hotel phone, I talked to Masimba back in Zimbabwe for hours, not once revealing my ordeal and never uttering it to anyone else after. He had not succeeded in physically raping me, but as he had pleasured himself with my body, I had felt emotionally and spiritually raped. I had, in fact, been sexually violated.

Weeks later, when my aunt scolded me on the phone for hiking up this man's hotel phone bill with the call I made to Zimbabwe, I just thought, *If only she knew, if only she knew.*

News of his death a year or so later came as pleasing to me. In the country and culture where I was raised, men like him get away with rape and murder every day because money is above the law. I knew his death meant another girl would not be subjected to the humiliation and degradation that I had been subjected to by him. I was not the first and surely not his last victim.

PART two

Breaking Rules.

SEVEN
An African Girl Adrift in America

After I had the money, I went to a travel agent and bought a ticket to Omaha, Nebraska. I headed to stay with a friend of a friend of my aunt's. "They are such good people," my aunt had said. "You will enjoy life in America."

After missing my first booked flight out of Gatwick, I bid farewell to my new friends and was early as a standby on my flight to America. This time, I had only my backpack with me. I told myself I would soon return to England. Sure that I had secured a place in nursing school, I left all my belongings with Tinazvo.

On this American Airline flight, I noticed the vast distinction between American and British people. The American flight attendants were so friendly and smiled with ease, unlike their British counterparts. With my visitor's visa, I was stamped into the great land that is America. The confusion that came with noticing iced tea in vending machines, and then wondering where one would heat the tea up to drink it, now makes me realize how backward I was.

On arrival at Eppley Airfield in Omaha, Nebraska, on July 1, 1999, I did not find the girl with whom I was to stay waiting for me, like she had promised on our last phone conversation before I boarded my flight. After waiting an hour, I gave Tsitsi a call.

"I'll be there shortly" was the response I got. I had no reason to think she wouldn't show up; we had arranged this in great detail over weeks. When another hour went by, I called again and suggested I take a cab, since I had some American dollars on me. She agreed and gave me the address once again. I flagged a cab outside the airport and told the cabdriver I wanted to go to South Twenty-Fourth Street. He told me it was about a twenty-minute ride. He inquired about my accent, so on our way I explained where I was from and that I was here just for a visit.

I arrived at my destination, paid the driver, and knocked on the door to the apartment number written in my pocket diary. Tsitsi opened the door, seemingly half asleep. I went in and sat on the only sofa in the room. She said she'd see me tomorrow, and where I sat was exactly where I spent the night. No offer of a pillow or even a blanket.

The following day, I was awakened by the shrill crying of a child. Upon further investigation, I found a baby boy about six months of age alone on the bed in Tsitsi's bedroom. I called out for Tsitsi, but she did not respond. I picked up the baby and took him to the kitchen, where I started hunting for anything that resembled a bottle and anything that resembled milk. I didn't find a bottle and I didn't find baby formula. I did find a pint of regular milk in the fridge, which I poured into a plastic cup. I warmed it in the dirty microwave and proceeded to feed the crying child.

I looked for nappies, but found none, except for a disposable diaper under the bed. I changed the baby and waited. As noon approached, I attempted to go outside with the baby, but the humidity and heat of the July Midwest weather hit me in the face. It knocked the wind out of me, leaving me unable to breathe and forcing me to retreat back into the shelter of the apartment.

I started to panic. I just got here and this woman I've only known over the past few weeks by phone just left her baby without giving me any warning and without leaving the things necessary for me to care for this child—the most basic being food. I had been left with no other choice but to cook the only packet I saw in the freezer, which said Salisbury steak. I'd never heard of it, but I decided to put it in the oven to cook it, not knowing it was already cooked and only needed heating up.

Somehow avoiding setting the place on fire, since I put it into the oven in its paper container, I managed to make a meal for me and my new buddy to share. I mashed his bites up the best I could. Finally, at around five in the evening, I heard a key turn in the door and Tsitsi walked in. I was furious with her. I asked her how she could just leave a baby and not even tell me, and to leave no milk for the child or nappies. She didn't think it was a big deal and told me some lie about her boyfriend, Randal, supposedly letting her down by not taking the baby to day care.

By the end of the first week, it was clear that I had come all the way to America to be Tsitsi's babysitter. Each day she left and left me to care for her child. I had no means of communicating with anyone. Her phone only called locally, so there was no way I could get a hold of my aunt back in Zimbabwe. I kept thinking that I had a two-week return ticket to England; so if all else failed, I would head back there.

The heat in this place was unbearable. I had never experienced so much humidity. For two long weeks, I stayed mostly inside, dependent on Tsitsi for everything. Then on the second weekend, she took me along to visit her sister, who lived in North Omaha. As soon as Tsitsi was out of hearing distance, her sister started questioning me about where I had come from, how long I had stayed with Tsitsi, and how I had even known Tsitsi in the first place. I answered truthfully and, without her saying it, I could tell she was worried.

When it was time to leave, Tsitsi's sister, who had four kids herself, asked Tsitsi if I could stay behind and help with the kids, who were now out of school for the summer break. I would have protested, but after two weeks in Tsitsi's lonely apartment, talking to a baby, anything would have been a much-needed break. I was happy to stay with these people.

As soon as Tsitsi left, her sister told me that she was afraid she and her husband would have to find ways to help me, as they didn't think Tsitsi would take the initiative. In the week I stayed with them, they took me to Council Bluffs, Iowa, where they helped me apply for a Social Security card as a means of obtaining a driver's license. My return ticket to England would expire without ever being used. As soon as my Social Security card came to the post box Tsitsi's sister's husband owned, he drove me to a place called Millard Good Samaritan, where he helped me fill out a form that would enroll me in a CNA (certified nursing assistant) class at the facility.

I had come as a visitor, but Tsitsi knew how to fix the Social Security card so it wouldn't show that it was not intended for work or study. I was very innocent when I got here, and I felt completely stuck with nowhere to turn and nowhere to go. I didn't know there was any other way. I just came here and started doing the things that those I was living with suggested I do.

At the time, I thought it was the only way. Truthfully, I thought every foreign person had to survive this way. I wasn't even aware that there could be any other options. At age nineteen, I really didn't know much about international affairs, and especially about the immigration laws of this country! I simply operated out of fear and sincerely believed that those who were helping me knew what was best. I thought at the time that they had my best interest at heart.

I was interviewed by the HR person and got hired. So on August 16, 1999, I began working at Good Samaritan, first taking the CNA class and then staying there for another nine years.

I soon befriended a girl from my CNA class who was only sixteen and had just had a baby. She was now taking the class so she could work and support her child, for the father was also a young boy. Jennifer was my first true friend in America and soon she was giving me rides back and forth from the facility. I no longer waited for hours for Tsitsi to show up when she felt like it. I started off making six dollars or so an hour, but it was something. I slowly started opening up to Jennifer, especially about my living conditions. I told her about how I just could not trust this person I was living with, but how at the same time I was indebted to her, since she was the one who gave me a place to stay.

Tsitsi was hard to get along with. Her life was chaotic and unorganized, and I just couldn't make my family back home understand the situation I was in. Tsitsi soon invited one of her cousins to come and live with her as well. Her name was Grace, and her moving into this apartment was my salvation. Even with being related to Tsitsi, Grace also felt her cousin was very unstable and hard to get along with. When Tsitsi made a trip back home, Grace and I changed the lease to our names, for we had been the ones making the rent and paying the bills for a long time now.

When Tsitsi returned, she was furious to learn of what we had done. I was scared about what she might do in retaliation. I had gone along on her crazy nights when she went after her son Tinashe's father and wanted to seek revenge for him leaving her and finding another girl to be with. She was angry because she had, in fact, paid his way here and had taken care of him while he attended school. She would make a scene at his apartment, demanding that he start taking care of his son. Robert and his girlfriend would just stand there, not knowing what to do with the crazy woman. I would just stand in silence, embarrassed by her behavior.

When I went to work the next day after the lease change, the HR person approached me and told me that someone had left a rather confusing message on her phone. She wanted me to listen to it. I followed her to her office and listened. Tsitsi had left her a message that simply said the HR woman had to look at my passport. My heart raced. I did not know what the HR person would say when I got off the phone, but she held the phone and said, "Should I delete it then?" I nodded yes, and that was the end of it.

After I told Grace about this, she suggested we move somewhere else. This way, Tsitsi would have nothing to do with our new place. We moved to a town called Papillion, way west of our current residence. This neighborhood was much quieter and much closer to our place of work. I had gone to apply to attend college at Bellevue University, with the hope that they could then transfer my visa into an F-1 student visa. At first, they told me they could and then said the expiration of my six months was too late for them to do so. And just like that, I was living without a status.

At first, I was very alarmed and upset that I had come to this country so ill prepared. I had not been treated well, and I had to work real hard for everything I had.

I was nineteen.

I was a kid.

For the past year, I had fended for myself so far away from home and from any assistance. Now, with my predicament, I simply had to do whatever I could to survive. I shopped for all my clothes at the Goodwill thrift stores and bought all my shoes only at discount shops, even though they never felt comfortable with the kind of work I did, which required standing for long periods of time.

Strangely, I still thought and felt like I was living large. After all, compared to how I had lived in England, this life I now had in America seemed much better. At work, I soon took the Medication Aide course, which allowed me to administer medication and increased my pay by a dollar an hour. After my CNA class, my pay had also increased, so I was making close to eleven dollars an hour.

At work, I met a guy named Darren, who was identical to Patrick Swayze. I never thought in a million years this handsome white guy would want to be anything more than friends with me. I saw myself as just an African girl, with a shaved head. At first, Darren just gave me rides home. Soon, though, he would start to come in and hang out for a little bit, maybe have a beer. Then one day it happened. While we wrestled on the floor, he kissed me.

We tried not to show our relationship at work. Darren helped me get my first car. It was a total piece of crap, with no heat. I would freeze that first winter on the nightly drive home from working the evening shift. As soon as I got home, I would turn on the stove to high and let my fingers melt at the red heat. It was so painful as they unfroze. After the brakes went completely out on me, Darren took me to a car lot, where I got a white Ford Probe. Compared to my first car, this one was like a Ferrari. It ran good; it had a stereo. Most important, it had heat and defrosting capability, so I could actually drive with the windows up and not freeze on the days it snowed sometimes six to eight inches.

I still communicated with my high-school love, Masimba, but my best friend, Thoko, had told me of his many girlfriends he was collecting with his new bank job. As a result of that—and other subconscious reasons—I had lost interest.

Darren was very sweet to me; and after so much time had elapsed from my drunken experience in Masimba's bedroom, I was now ready to give sex a try again. After all, I was now twenty years old. I was living on my own and paying my own bills. I had spent the night at Darren's place, which he shared with his uncle. Darren was about twenty-two and already had a child. His child lived with Darren's ex-girlfriend, so I never met the little boy. It was somewhat weird to be dating someone who was a parent, but I had learned in this country that wasn't so unusual.

The first time I made love to this Patrick Swayze look-alike, I found it enjoyable, but not mind-blowing. I had broken my rule: I wasn't married yet. I had experienced everything else, so I finally gave in to this. I knew I never wanted to wind up pregnant by accident, so I was very adamant about protection at all times. I was getting very comfortable in this relationship, when, out of nowhere, Darren informed me that he had decided to get back with the mother of his son, mostly for his son's sake.

I wanted to plead with him, to beg him not to leave me. The words, however, would not come. I just looked at him as he told me of how one day I would find someone who was meant for me, and blah, blah, blah. I was hurt. I didn't expect it to end so soon. Working with him became awkward. He was now distant, but then he quit Good Sam altogether and vanished from the face of the earth.

I was now convinced that maybe the person I was intended to be with was Masimba. I did not realize at this tender age that it was okay to be alone, so I refocused my attention on our relationship. We started communicating more, writing often, sending photos back and forth. Then we decided it was best if he tried to move to America to be with me. He would ask for money for all this stuff, like securing a visa and paying bills. In the meantime, I would work infinite double shifts, so I made sure to have the extra money to send him, as well as my family back home. When he said everything was in order, I forwarded him the money he said was needed for an air ticket—$1,500.

On the day he was to arrive, I waited eagerly at the airport, but he never came. Panicked, I went back to my apartment, loaded with calling cards, to try and find out what had happened. I would call his house, and they would say he was at work. I would call his work, and they would put me on hold, only to come back and say he was not in. One day, when someone at his house picked up the phone, I inquired about his trip to come and see me. They said they didn't know anything about a trip and that he had not mentioned he would be going anywhere. In fact, he was out, playing soccer, at that very moment.

I couldn't believe it. This guy had collected things from my relatives to bring to me—their wedding photos and gifts they wanted me to have. Masimba had taken these things, knowing that he never intended to come. He just wanted to take the money. After all these years of knowing this person, who had been my high-school sweetheart, with whom I had spent almost each day of the last two years of my high-school education, had now betrayed me for $1,500. I tried to get my money back; he would give me false reference numbers, until finally I gave up on ever getting my money back. I gave up on him forever. It took at least a year for me not to hurt over what had happened. Ironically, he had managed to lead me on and ultimately scam money out of me—just like the "Nigerian Prince" phishing scams that make people send money overseas in the hopes of getting a big reward in return.

I dated random guys, including Micky, who was my first friend Jennifer's ex-boyfriend. Call it loneliness. In all fairness, Jennifer and I had grown apart, but Micky had stuck around. He was there for me. He was a total bum, but I guess I was desperate.

I met the handsome pharmacy student Kevin while leaving a club one night. With his big house, way west in the better part of town, and his brand-new Infiniti, he seemed promising. After the 80mph drive around the curve on Q Street, I had to say my good-bye. Sure enough, the next time I met him, he had totaled his Infiniti and was now driving a Honda Accord.

Among my boyfriends was a guy from Zimbabwe who suffered from seizures, but he never prated about it. Marvin fell over one day while we waited in line for a pizza. He was so ashamed that he suffered from this disability, as if it was something he had chosen.

Then there was the only African-American man I ever tried to date, until he showed up with bandages to his inner elbows after donating plasma in order to take me out on a date. I dropped him off at his mom's house that night and never returned any of his phone calls again. He didn't have a car, so I knew there was no way he could show up at my door. Each time he was over at my place, when he left, some DVD of mine would be missing. I said good riddance to that.

It took me some time to understand that this guy was not a reflection of all African Americans, but my experience with him made me gain insight into how and why African Americans are somehow viewed with suspicion or are stereotyped.

I soon realized that my perception of my surroundings didn't match that of African Americans'. I didn't see the world divided into black and white people, as they did. Most African Americans I came across seemed to view white people as "them," like they were not the same and could never be. My best friends growing up had been my white next-door neighbors. I guess coming from a country where black people were the majority, and without a deep history of racial segregation, I didn't feel inherently different from white people.

I didn't understand why African Americans spoke completely different English from Caucasians. I didn't understand why so many African Americans lived in seemingly poor neighborhoods. Why didn't they utilize all the benefits and advantages of being an American?

I always thought that if I had been lucky enough to be born in this country, I would have made sure I took advantage of every opportunity that I had. These days, however, I realize that it is much easier to be judgmental when you have an outsider's view, when you have experienced a different life and have lived elsewhere.

Interestingly, I now find it hard to understand some of the things that most Africans do, because I have now lived away from Africa for so long and carry an outsider's view. I also, now, better understand the disparities within race that have caused African Americans to lag behind, how those disparities are engraved into everything including the justice system. I am alarmed by the mere fact that even though studies show that blacks and whites use illegal drugs at about the same rates, African Americans are disproportionately imprisoned for drug-related offenses; I have come to comprehend how just that one statistic can infiltrate and affect an entire generation of people.

Luckily, I had great African-American role models, like Pam Pete, who was one of my supervisors at work, to offset my prejudicial feelings. Still, there was an internal great divide from the way I viewed the world and the way Africans Americans seemed to see it. Our environments do indeed shape us.

Now, finally somewhat settled, the biggest thing I wanted to do for myself was have a really great twenty-first birthday party. I invited everyone to my apartment on the night of my birthday and that day I legally bought a boatload of alcohol. It ranged from a keg, which could get about a hundred people drunk, to margarita mixes and all kinds of tequilas and vodkas. My friend Nicky prepared all the food: greens and neck bones, Mac-n-Cheese and fried chicken.

Nicky was the only African-American woman I had befriended in all my time in the States. I admit that I found this disappointing. When I had left England, I had hoped that I would have more in common with this group of people, with whom I shared an ancestry, but this was not the case. There was that cultural chasm separating us. My views of the world and even of America were so dissimilar from the ones of most African Americans I had encountered.

Nicky worked with me and lived in the projects with her six children. At the tender age of twelve, Nicky birthed her oldest child—the pregnancy was the result of sexual experimentation, she had told me. This first daughter would regrettably also be a teenage mom, having her first child at fourteen, forcing Nicky to be a grandparent before the age of thirty!

Nicky had such a cool air about her. She didn't judge me and was not intimidated by my ways. The way I spoke, which was different and proper due to the British background I grew up with, made me sound different. At times I felt like my vocal inflections intimidated other people. I also am just a very loud and opinionated person, which I think takes some people aback.

We were buds, and her name for me was "wholdi," which is basically slang for "good friend." On this day, I started drinking at about eleven in the morning. By the time people started arriving at four o'clock, I was inebriated. The music was loud, and more and more people kept showing up. "Dollar Bill," a guy from work, was supplying blunts to whoever wanted; soon, in the cramped space of my apartment, a cloud of smoke hung about, infecting everyone in the premises with an involuntary high. The cheap pool table I had in the kitchen had been moved to the living room and battles were taking place. One girl was so drunk and high that she was practically crawling on her hands and knees, unable to balance on her feet. Soon there was a knock on the door; and in the noise and rush of people I could not hear, but I was alerted by the scrambling. Some people were escaping outside to the patio; some had scurried into my bed and my roommate's bedroom. I knew at once that someone had called the police.

I staggered to the door. Waiting there was a black cop, and the first thing that came out of my mouth was "It's only because I'm black, isn't it? If a white person was having a party, you wouldn't show up!"

He could obviously tell I was drunk out of my mind. He tried to be polite and said, "Ma'am, all I need you to do is keep it down."

His politeness sobered me up a little, for I had answered the door ready for a fight. I thanked him for coming and reignited the party. I was hailed a heroine, and more drinking games began.

At some point, I passed out and woke up the next day in bed with a bucket full of vomit beside me. I was sick to my stomach, but content that the party was just what I had wanted it to be.

There was a danger looming, however, with this newfound freedom of being of legal age and therefore able to buy and drink whenever I wanted. Not too long after my party, I decided to go bowling with Samantha and Trish. We'd order one pitcher of alcohol after another, and I'm not even sure any of us ever picked up a bowling ball the entire time we were there. When it came time to leave, I demanded to drive, since I could tell the other two were so ravaged. Trying to get to Eighty-Fourth Street, ten minutes away from where we were, I ended up driving to 180th Street. I got in a car chase with some guys; and when I had made my way home, with only one turn left to go, I noticed the flashing lights of a police car in my rearview mirror. I pulled over, right next to my apartment, actually. I failed every sobriety test I was given and, without incident, I was arrested for DWI.

My cousin Timothy, who was living with me, had heard the commotion from where he was inside the apartment. As he approached the police cars, with his hands in his pockets, one of the cops drew out his gun and pointed it at him, demanding he remove his hands out of his pockets and put them up in the air. Timothy's jaw dropped as he did what he had been asked to do, while pleading the fact that I was his younger cousin and he wanted to find out what the problem was. After that incident, every time I heard a case of the police shooting an unarmed black man, it took me back to that night.

    I clearly remember the female cop, asking me about my accent and if I was a citizen. I responded by asking her if she was a racist, and that ended that inquiry abruptly. I had a gut instinct that raising the specter of "racism" would stop the questioning. Luckily, I was bailed out within about two hours, as the county jail was five minutes down the street. For the first time since taking my first drink of alcohol at fourteen, I was forced to think that maybe, just maybe, alcohol wasn't so great, after all. The rude awakening was yet to follow.

    In the next week, I received a notification that my driver's license would be suspended for six months. On a brighter note, I also had the option of taking a diversion course, which would help eliminate this first DWI, as long as I didn't get another one in the future. I was quick to enroll in this diversion program. The requirements were two AA meetings a week and one class, held once a week for six months, about the effects of drunk driving.

    That very week, I attended my first AA meeting. I found it bizarre the way everyone introduced themselves, "Hi, my name is such and such and I'm an alcoholic." *How strange,* I thought at the time, *I can't wait for this to be over so I can get my card signed and get out of here.* Then people started to share their stories of broken marriages, broken relationships, broken hope, and broken lives. I started to realize that they were not crazy, after all; they may have started off just like I had.

    When I attended the first class on the effects of drunk driving, I heard about groups, like MADD (Mothers Against Drunk Driving). I heard their testimonies of how in an instant some of them had lost innocent children to people just like me—people who didn't think for a second that drinking too much was a problem, or that drinking too much and then getting behind the wheel was a problem. I remember weeping in one class. I didn't want to become the person in these stories, the person who took an innocent person's life just for the sake of having fun.

From that day on, I made a solemn vow never to drink and then drive, for the price to pay was high. Even when no life was lost, it had cost me $500 to enroll in this program, plus about four hours of my week, each week for six months, all for one night of fun. After six months, my license was reissued, and drinking was never the same for me.

I knew I wanted to start going to college, but how could I? I was living without a status. One day, I took my chances. I went to the local community college, Metro, and tried to register to go to school. I knew I would have to lie. I filled out the form, lying where I felt necessary. I was told of the advisors who could help me choose classes. At the time, I was interested in psychology or maybe computer programming. After taking the assessment tests for the different subjects, since I had indicated that I had completed my high school abroad, I started attending classes. I took the basic requirements for most degree programs: English 101 and 102, algebra intermediate and college, psychology 101, computer fundamentals.

I felt alive! My essays in my English classes were always impressive, but not always honest. In my classes, I was astounded by how people from this country knew so little about many subjects. I always seemed to have the answer to questions that teachers asked. I seemed to be a know-it-all, when, in fact, the things I knew were basic, learned over a six-year period of high school back in Zimbabwe. Most surprising was my better knowledge of the history of America, but then again it had been my favorite subject back in high school. In order to get any attention from the young female history teacher, I had put in greater effort, researching things not asked for. The teacher had seemed intrigued with my interest on the subjects, and now it was paying off. I was working full-time and in school part-time. I was finally maturing.

My cousin Timothy was the first person from home to move to Omaha. I had sent him the application forms to Metropolitan Community College and he had been accepted and was granted an F-1 student visa. He stayed with me and Grace in our apartment and slept on the couch. Even though Timothy was somewhat of a distant cousin, it was good just to have someone who knew me from back home, someone who had seen me grow up and was actually sharing the same space as I was. As soon as he began working at Good Samaritan, he was soon dubbed "next of kin," as he was my only relative around.

From the very start, Timothy caused quite a stir with the ladies, especially the Caucasian ones. There was only one problem: He was a married man, with a beautiful wife and a son back in Zimbabwe. At first, he vowed to be true to his wife and child, no matter what. Then the letter from Lisa came, in which she said he was such a beautiful man. Then there was Tracy, a young married nurse, with a little boy. I warned them both, but to no avail. Tracy came with us to Kansas City on the pretense that Timothy and I were a couple. They were grown-ups and there was nothing I could personally do to stop them.

After our trip, Tracy's husband became very suspicious. Eventually she confessed that she indeed was having an affair with Timothy. When I drove to her house to get her, her husband had all her belongings on the front lawn and he was livid.

"Thank you so much for ruining my marriage" was what he said to me when I got there. In my mind, I was saying, *I don't think I see a penis on me!* It wasn't me, but they had used my name so much that he felt that I, too, was responsible.

As cars passed by, inquiring about the possibility of it being a garage sale, he would say, "No, my wife cheated on me."

Tracy got a divorce and continued this love affair with my cousin, who was close to bringing his own family over. I tried to talk to him about making sure at least he ended things with Tracy before bringing Zandie and Takunda over. My words fell on deaf ears. His wife and child would come, and he would continue the affair, until Zandie got a call from one of Tracy's friends, who could no longer see this go on.

Zandie demanded I take her to Tracy's place. When we got there, no one was home. As we got ready to leave, Timothy and Tracy arrived in the same car. If there had been a hole big enough to swallow him, Timothy would have jumped in it.

Zandie was enraged. She wanted to know how long it had been going on, and she wanted to know why. While Timothy promised to end it and make things right, Zandie stayed with him. What else could she do? She had just arrived here, with no job and no other place to go.

I may have judged her at first for staying with him, but then I knew how debilitating it was to be in a foreign country with no job and no money and dependent on someone else for existence. I had lived that plight so many times. Eventually, in their own way, they worked it out and had another son.

Timothy completed his bio/chemistry degree from the University of Nebraska and eventually moved to Canada, where permanent residence and citizenship were much easier to attain than in America. Today, Timothy is also a promising and talented musician.

EIGHT
Death Pays a Visit, but I Can't

Since I had left home, so many things had happened. The economy in Zimbabwe went from bad to worse, and my aunt Norma, who had kept a good job for many years, was forced to resign and pursue other things. She decided to go to England to get a master's degree in micro finance in the hopes of starting up a financing company. Her move led to Nyasha, Tapiwa, and Tashinga being left in the care of their father, Adam. The task of having the kids, without my aunt around, proved too much for him. The kids would go days without groceries, or he would send them to buy groceries on foot and they would not buy the things that were needed. My aunt's once-loving family was starting to crumble, and so was her marriage.

My grandmother's health also began to deteriorate. When she got too sick, my aunt had to return home. My grandmother passed away after her daughter's return on September 26, 2002. She was eighty-four years old. The death of my aunt Lucy, her oldest child, shortly before had been too much for her to take.

One of the most difficult things about living in a country illegally is not being able to fly back home at times like this, when someone so dear to you passes.

That very year, on Valentine's Day, I was sitting in a restaurant, enjoying a fine seafood meal, when I received news that my aunt Lucy had passed. In shock, I doubled over, almost choking on my salad. I cried so loud and hard, creating a scene without even realizing it.

It was excruciatingly hard not being able to attend my grandmother's funeral. I did manage to send $500 to help buy the casket she was to be buried in. When the long-distance call came in, I heard, *"Ambuya vashaya,"* meaning "your grandmother is dead." In that instant, my life with her flashed before my eyes. I was overcome with sudden grief, debilitated by the disbelief of it all.

I could picture her standing by the bathroom window, like she often did in my aunt's Mt. Pleasant home, calling my name, "Wheety girl! Wheety!" I would try to hide behind a tree in our backyard so I wouldn't yet again have to help her with scrubbing her back, something I had done for as long as I could remember. Then, out of guilt, I would come out of hiding and run inside. Still out of breath, I would take the soapy sponge and sit on the edge of the tub. I would start scrubbing, making sure I did a good job the first time, for she was sure to point out a spot I had missed. This was such a loving and delightful act. She always looked so relaxed, as if my scrubbing was some type of therapeutic massage. It melted away all the stresses of her life, all the hardships she had faced from the time she worked as a maid for the whites, mistreated and on occasion beaten for stealing things she never stole, and having to keep her children inside all day, for they were not allowed on the property. All the years of working on the land, planting and harvesting, all by hand without the help of any machinery, took its toll on her. But none of those things had erased even a dash of her beauty.

I held the phone as my tears flooded everything around me. I should have treasured my moments with her more, treasured every second I had spent in this woman's presence. On cold and rainy days I would come home from school, soaked and drenched, and she would fill the tub with hot water, while she made me some hot tea. I should have thanked her endlessly, for the shielding she gave me when my surrogate parents wanted to scold me and she vowed to leave if they did. I should have been grateful for the many times she defended me, even when she knew I was wrong, for always taking my side—no matter what the argument was.

I should have thanked her for her genes, which gave me my high cheekbones and full lips. These were gifts she passed on to my mother, my mother to me, and now I have passed on to my children. We all have cheekbones and full lips that undoubtedly belong to Milka Murehwa.

I should have been grateful to her for the gift of life. I might not have emerged from my grandmother's womb, but it was because of her that I was alive and well today. It's because of her that I've gotten to where I am fearlessly and was able to brave every storm that has come my way.

As I had never seen a man by her side in all her life, she truly showed me the strength and power that a woman possesses—the strength and power that I possess as well. It would take days of sorrow and tears with every inquisition about her death in order for me to say it was okay. It took time for me to say maybe she was in a better place, and to realize that she would want me to mourn only for a short while and then move on. So I did that, convinced that I now, for sure, had a guardian angel.

NINE
Meeting an Unpredictable Prince

It was around this time that I met a very handsome fellow. While I was out on the town with friends one night, Ted walked by me. Then he stopped and gave me a second look. I caught him in the act; and to show I was not the least bit annoyed, I had put an inviting smile on my face. To my surprise, he invited himself over to where I was sitting. He introduced himself while looking me up and down, not at all trying to hide that he was checking me out.

His skin looked bronzed in the dim light. He had a Kangol hat on, flipped to the side, a blue polo neck Tommy Hilfiger sweater, and baggy jeans. I let him know my name. He grabbed my hand, pulling me in the direction of the dance floor, which was packed with bodies moving rhythmically to the sound of the hip-hop beat. On the dance floor, he pulled me real close, as if he had known me forever. I started to giggle, surprised at this stranger's boldness. He danced much better than I had expected. He moved well, had a way to make himself seem like the only person on that dance floor. I was impressed.

After the third song, he finally tired. While he wiped the sweat off his brow, he suggested we sit down for a drink. Hey, I wasn't looking for anything or anyone that night, but he sure had my attention then. He told me he was thirty years old; to which, I cringed inside a little. I later found out that he had lied to me about his age. He was even older than that: He was actually thirty-one when I met him! I had just turned twenty-two that January. I had dated older guys, but none that much older. Then I looked at his face and he didn't look a day older than twenty. His body looked perfect, even under the heavy sweater, so I ignored the thought in my head. By the end of the night, we were talking of meeting again the very next day. Maybe for breakfast, he implied.

We set a date for brunch at Village Inn for the very next day. My aunt Norma was in town, however, finally managing to visit me for the first time. We had planned to go shopping at the mall that next day, so I would have to find some way out of that shopping trip. On the following day at the mall, my "date" appointment time was nearing. I told my aunt I had to run and do something real quick. Meeting with a man I had just met at the only time she was in town was not going to sound too good. So, off I went to Village Inn to meet Mr. Prince Charming from the previous night.

I arrived there, a little unsettled and nervous at the same time. I walked in and requested "a place for two, please." I was at the booth, waiting for his arrival, but after ten minutes the waiter returned and asked if I would like to go ahead and order. Embarrassed, I ordered just a hot tea. I had a telephone number to reach him, but no cell phone at the time. I sat and waited and waited. After an hour, it was clear he simply was not showing up.

Disappointed, I rejoined my aunt at the mall, where she immediately sensed my mood was off.

"Everything okay?" she asked.

I nodded yes, but inside I was boiling. I had only been stood up once before, back in high school. At least, Masimba had the decency to show up even after the movie was over. On my way back to the mall, I had ripped up the piece of paper he had scribbled his number on, telling myself it was a sign.

When I got back to my apartment, I checked my voice mail and this person had left me seven messages: "I'm so sorry, baby. I got caught up doing something. I need to see you. Today, if possible."

Prince Charming was alive, after all, but what was up with the calling me "baby"? I took a long pause after hearing the messages, just a little spooked. Despite my gut instinct, I called the number on my caller ID. He immediately started to apologize and to plead as soon as he heard my voice. I agreed to meet him that evening at Applebee's right in my neighborhood.

Yet again, I had to come up with an excuse to Aunt Norma as to why I had to be gone again for a little while. When I got there, he was already waiting. In the light of day, he looked much lighter than I remembered. It was clear that he was Caucasian and not mixed or Hispanic like I had assumed. He was wearing a hat, T-shirt, and jeans. As the waiter walked us to our table, I spotted my roommate, Grace, eating with her mother, who was also visiting from Zimbabwe. I shyly walked past them, knowing there would be questions later.

We sat down and he touched my hand across the table. It felt weird, so I pulled away. I began small talk, asking him what happened earlier. He simply said something came up and he couldn't make it. I then asked him if he always wore a hat, and he said yes.

I asked, "Can you take it off so I can see your face better?"

When he obliged, he revealed a balding center, which instantly added ten years to the face that had looked twenty a second ago. I tried to act unmoved; I asked if he had kids. He answered two, and "They stay with their mother, and I get them on the weekends."

Well, I thought, *it can't be too bad.* I had dated Darren, who had a son, and that went okay. Why panic, right?

He then did something so very unusual. When the waiter came to get our orders, he took out a wad of hundred-dollar bills from his pocket. They were wrapped in a rubber band and he put them on the table. He returned them to his pocket after the waiter and I had both had a stare.

We finished eating and he then informed me that he had to go out of town for the weekend. He proceeded to make me promise that I would not go out and meet someone else that weekend. How bizarre, but I just laughed it off, finding it comical. Outside he asked me to sit in his truck with him for a little bit. I agreed; I guessed he wanted to make out. His kisses were careless and desperate. He was holding me much too tight. It did nothing for me.

I pushed away a little, to get some air, and said that I should get going. I got out of his truck and headed to my car. On the drive back to my place, I wasn't sure what to think. Sure, he was good-looking, but "bald" suddenly jumped out of nowhere. The kids bit? I was not so sure about that. He seemed to have money and was full of conversation, and he seemed to be completely taken with me.

The following week, after Aunt Norma had returned to England, I invited him over to my place to hang out. When I initially suggested a movie to him, he said he didn't go to movies with girls he didn't know much about. Boy, this guy was something! The other day, he wanted to swallow my face, and now I was too much of a stranger to watch a movie with.

Why is it that when God throws us all these signs, somehow we just seem to miss them? I started dating Ted Browner. More than any other guy I had been with, he was starved for my attention. He called and wanted to be called whenever we were not together. When we went clubbing, he was very possessive. He would become easily frustrated when a guy simply said hello to me.

Then one day, after much convincing, he agreed for me to go over to his place. He lived in a basement apartment. He had a single old couch placed awkwardly in the corner of his living room. His sink was full of rotting dishes. His bed was invisible under the weight of both clean and dirty clothes. There were random pieces of children's clothes on the floor. His bathroom looked like it had never been cleaned, and the only television set in the whole place measured a mere seven inches and looked like it was out of the 1950s.

My first reaction was to turn around and run, but instead I heard myself saying, "Why don't we clean up the place first?" I spent half the day scrubbing, folding, sweeping, and doing laundry. If I had to sit in this place even for half a minute, I had to try to get it clean.

His roommate, Lance, slept in the living room on the couch. The heavy odor of maleness in that room was strong enough to make my eyes water. With Ted's help, I cleaned the best I could. By evening, the bed looked neat, with fresh sheets washed at last, after God knows how long. The dishes were put away and the living room was now sanitary. After about three weeks of being together, we spent our first night at his place.

As I cleaned, I had seen random pictures of different children. One was on his windowsill—a boy of mixed race, with his exact face; and pinned on his wall was the photo of a smiling little Caucasian girl. These pictures were separate from the obvious ones of a mixed woman with him and two kids in some pictures. These, I guessed, were pictures of his ex, the one with whom he had the two kids. But then who were the other ones? It would take me three more times of visiting his apartment before I would have the courage to ask about those kids.

"Oh, that's my son in Sioux City," he said.

Okay, I thought we had the discussion about kids, and I thought you had told me you had only two. This was the thought that crossed my mind. For the time being, I let it go.

A month into our relationship, I would see another side to Ted. He had come along to play basketball with me, my cousin Timothy, and Samantha's boyfriend, Chiku. At the basketball court, we met up with Chris and Billy from work. I took the initiative and divided the group into teams. I was on Timothy and Chiku's team, while Ted would be on Chris and Billy's team. I could hang with the big boys when it came to basketball, and it showed as I would slip and slide, make fake passes, and shoot at long range.

As the game went on, and my team was winning, everyone could tell Ted was getting irritated. It was competitive; but to the rest of us who had played together often, it was just a game. After removing his shirt and angrily tossing it on the ground, as to be more defensive, it was very clear that this guy was a sore loser. At the end of the game, all hell broke loose.

He cursed at me, yelling, "You bitch, cunt, filthy whore! Why did you have to be on their team, huh? Why? Why couldn't you be on my team? What a bitch this is!"

I stood, stock-still in my tracks, unable to move from where I was. All the guys were just as paralyzed. No one said a word for a few seconds, not even Timothy. His jaw was almost all the way to the ground.

Timothy made the first move toward me, motioning me to come with him. "Let's go, sis" was all he could summon up.

We stepped into my Ford Explorer, which I had just purchased, and drove home, leaving Ted to walk. Timothy said nothing, and I said nothing. I had never been called a "bitch," "cunt," or "whore" to my face in my whole life. I didn't even know how to process it. It stung so deep. I'm sure that getting whipped with rope made of cowhide that was soaked in salt, like I had often seen the farmers do to their cows when I was growing up, would have felt less painful. What a monster!

And while I sat in quiet, behind my closed door at home, he knocked. With tears running down my face now, I asked him what he wanted.

He responded with a voice full of tears. "I'm so sorry. I don't know what got into me. Please, please, forgive me."

His cries got even louder. I opened the door and he entered and just wept. He cried like I had never seen a man cry before. He even lay down on the carpet, curled into a fetal position, and just wept.

Now I was even more confused. I was hurt by his words, but why was he acting like his mother had just died? He kept repeating "sorry," until I found myself reaching down to the carpet, where he lay, and comforted him. Now I was the one saying, "I'm sorry." His face was now beet red; tears were running down his cheeks, like a water main break, and snot was falling out of his nose. Wow, and I had thought my lonely cries as a kid were intense. This was serious.

After witnessing such a performance, where would I get the energy to give him my speech about how I wanted him out of my life?

After this incident, many followed. There were some fights about his kids—four that I now knew about. He would get angry and push and shove. Then one day, he choked me, putting both his hands around my neck, squeezing and then letting go. Should I have been surprised? In passing, he had told me of how after an argument he had choked Zoey, the one with the two kids.

By the way, Zoey never brought their kids around, except for one occasion when I was over at his apartment. The little blond boy and younger brunette girl had run into his apartment, and their mom, who resembled Halle Berry, walked in after. She had sat in a corner, not saying much. I kept myself busy, pretending to be doing dishes in the kitchen. Ted had chased the cute kids around, trying to capture a photograph of them. I had left for the grocery store to give them some privacy. When I returned, Zoey was sitting on the steps outside, sobbing. I ignored her and went in while he bid them farewell. That had been their only visit, which I knew of.

After the choking incident, he begged me not to call the police; and, just like that, he began crying hysterically. In his anger and in the way he would regret afterward, it was almost as if he were a demon possessed. Then his conscious self would return and he would be ashamed.

Ted took trips to Sioux City often, which I knew by now were to see his other two boys. One of the boys he knew for sure was his, and the other he was sure was not his. Both were by the same mom.

I struggled with the fact that he had these children by these different women. I also was bothered by the fact that he never truly revealed why these previous relationships ended. I would have gladly shared about my past relationships; but whenever I made an attempt, Ted would become frustrated, telling me that he preferred to think of me as "never before touched" and "pure." This was mind-boggling, since he had a team of kids and I couldn't even say I had dated other guys.

After four months of being together, Ted became insistent that we get married. He had suggested we move in together so he would not have to pay rent for his own place. Because of the sporadic nature of his construction job, I had paid his rent already on one occasion. I had helped him pay bills and often gave him lunch money. Because of the way I was raised, living with a man I was not married to would not do. I also never wanted to make the mistake of getting pregnant out of wedlock.

At times, things were very good between Ted and me. He was very caring and overly loving toward me. He wrote me poetry and always told me he loved me. I had opened up to him about my childhood and he had cried with me. We shared a lot of emotional moments. So even though he had a temper and a past, when he proposed, I gladly said yes.

He moved in with me, and we couldn't salvage much of any of the things he owned. We kept the bigger TV, which I had convinced him to buy, and his chest of drawers. We threw out everything else.

While I was busy throwing out physical junk and objects, I was also throwing out my own personal doubts and hidden instincts. Perhaps the biggest, silent struggle for me to be living with a man under my roof stemmed from the fact that I had never actually enjoyed being intimate with a man. Even way back in my high-school days, when I had some of the most amazing relationships, they worked best when they were platonic. Being under the same roof with Ted meant that I would have to develop some really good skills of avoidance when it came to sex and intimacy.

More often than not, I hated myself after sexual encounters with him. It was a reaction I really didn't understand. I struggled to comprehend why it always felt so forced, even when I felt like I wanted it.

Why was it that anytime I had ever been intimate with a man, it felt like a violation?

TEN
Reasons to Tie the Knot

On his insistence, on January 15, 2003, we got married at the Sarpy County Courthouse. Nicole stood as my witness and an older gentleman named Vernon, who later died of cancer, stood as Ted's witness. So many things went through my mind as I sat in a bathroom stall before entering the courtroom. I could hear myself crying inside.

I thought of how I never intended to marry someone like him. I had grown up without a family of my own. If I was to have one, I had told myself, it wouldn't be with someone who already had one.

I thought about his many abuses toward me.

I thought about our age difference.

I thought about the fact that he didn't have a college degree and how I was determined to have one someday.

With sorrow, I also thought about the time he had stood by me when I had felt sick for several weeks, aching with general malaise and swollen lymph nodes. When the doctor had asked me if I had ever taken an HIV test, I was overcome with worry. In the days I awaited the results, Ted had assured me everything would be okay. After dialing the number and entering my code, and hearing negative for type 1 and negative for type 2, I had been relieved and glad I had someone there for support.

When I thought of all these things, I thought of the biggest difference marrying him would make in my life. I could finally adjust my status and live here legally. It was this thought that squashed the doubting Thomas that had been dancing around in my head.

I wiped my eyes dry and walked into the courtroom, taking my place beside him and saying, "I do." Immediately after, I felt a great deal of sadness inside as if a part of me had died. However, I knew my family back home would be so proud.

ELEVEN
A Temporary Encounter with Paradise

Back in England, Aunt Norma had brought the kids to stay with her. Nyasha, her oldest daughter, remained in Zimbabwe because she had become a handful since becoming a teenager. Tapiwa and Tashinga were now living with her.

After having last seen my little "sister" when she was three, I was absolutely thrilled when my mother suggested a visit to America with both kids in tow. Tapiwa was now fourteen and baby Tashinga was eight.

My new husband had started a small-scale roofing company with a guy named Philly, who had come from the West Coast. Ted was finally starting to make money after having been laid off and jobless for the first three months of our marriage. It was during this buildup to Tashinga's visit that I came home one day and was surprised to find the piggy bank, which I was filling up for Tashinga's arrival, empty. Ted had taken the money; I didn't ask.

My family arrived. On a lot of days, Aunt Norma and I discussed the collapse of a once-thriving Zimbabwean economy, political unrest, and everything else that was occurring and making being Zimbabwean almost unbearable. I knew from the money she had often asked for while back in England that she was struggling with the kids and trying to get a master's degree. I suggested she leave the kids behind with me. There were schools within walking distance from where I lived, and I knew from research that any child under the age of eighteen was entitled to attend school, regardless of immigration status.

When my aunt expressed worry about my own status, I assured her that I would have it corrected soon; at that time, I would get the kids' status adjusted as well. I had seen an immigration lawyer regarding my case. He had advised me that my status was adjustable and had given me a list of the paperwork that I needed to return in order for him to begin the processing. I also needed to bring him $2,500 as a down payment. I was very pleased. He wanted my passport and I-94, which I knew I had, my immunization record, which I knew I could have sent for from back home, and a physical completed by a doctor permitted to do immigration examinations. From my husband, the lawyer needed a birth certificate, tax documents for the past three years, and a divorce decree, if he had ever been previously married.

I had approached Ted about the adjusting of my status shortly after we had gotten married. When I had gone back to him asking for the documents needed, he informed me that he had never in his life seen his birth certificate. He would ask his mother about its whereabouts and get back to me. In the time I had been with him, he had never filed for taxes. So I waited for his share of documents; days turned into weeks, which turned into months. (Eventually this waiting would evolve into years.)

Norma returned to England, leaving her children in my care. Adjusting to this new role was not easy. Trying to play the "sister" role while playing the "mother" role was much harder than I expected it to be. This was mostly because their mother was never happy with any of the rules I had put in place for Tapiwa and Tashinga. If I said the TV had to be off at eleven o'clock on school nights, it was *you never let her kids watch TV.* If I bought a bike for Tapiwa to ride to school, so I could make it to work on time, then it was *you're making him ride a bike to school.*

Clothes needed to be bought; school lunches needed to be paid for; we managed. Surprisingly, Ted was very good with both of them. He was much more patient than I was, maybe because he had been a parent for a while.

Close to our first anniversary, I asked Aunt Norma to return so that Ted and I could go on a vacation. We had never taken a honeymoon, so this would be it. She agreed to come and stay with the kids, but then Ted was annoyed that we had to pay for her airfare. Plus, I always had to be sending money to her, and yet we were taking care of the kids.

A day before Norma was to arrive, we had gone out and I did

not like the bar that Ted had brought me to. He was angry to have to leave and became very agitated. As the argument accelerated in his truck, he had punched me in the face with one hand, while he drove with the other. I had attempted to punch him back, which made him even more infuriated. Like a madman, he veered the truck into oncoming traffic. I started to scream, while he was yelling something about not being afraid to die. He slammed into a pay phone on the sidewalk, slid out of the road and into an empty parking lot, where he then told me to get out. As soon as I opened the door, he used his foot to push me out and he sped off.

Within a few minutes, a police car arrived. Someone who had witnessed the incident had called the police. The policewoman was very nice. She asked me to sit in the front of the police car, which I did. Calmly she asked if I wanted to press charges, and I said no. I was so used to his violence and abuse that I had never thought of pressing charges.

Along with that acceptance of my abuse, I also worried about the consequences of my illegal status if I started to involve the law. I had so much fear about so much! In a weird way, I had felt safer before being married. Now, after tying the knot, I had exposed my illegal status to someone who could use it against me. I became more aware of the fact that I was illegal, once I was married, and knew that my husband now knew it, too. His knowing gave me a reason to tolerate his abuse as time went on. The police officer engaged in small talk with me, until I got to my apartment. Then I ran upstairs, to where Timothy lived, and told him and Zandie the story.

They didn't say much, having lived in the apartment above us since Ted had moved in with me. Grace had moved out, and they had heard way too many fights. Looking back, I wish somebody had said something, anything. My cousin and his wife had never intervened in all the times they had witnessed his verbal, emotional, and physical abuse toward me. I shouldn't have been surprised. After all, silence and a deep, cultural reluctance to discuss bad events—a willful decision to remain quiet about uncomfortable situations—were all a part of our shared heritage.

Ted did not come home, and the next day Norma was to arrive. I started frantically looking for him, for I did not want my aunt to know that all was not well. I found him at a friend's house. He asked if I had filed charges; I said no; he followed me home. By the time Norma arrived, we picked her up at the airport, even holding hands, seemingly more in love than ever.

That week, Ted and I left for Hawaii. Just getting out of the winter cold of Nebraska was refreshing. The journey was long, but upon arrival—receiving fresh-smelling, purple-and-pink floral necklaces—it was worth the journey. We were shuttled to our hotel and our room had a direct view of the Waikiki beach.

Yes, he had almost killed the both of us a few days ago. However, being here now, in this beautiful, paradise-like city, with palm tree–lined roads, with an endless ocean view, which was magnificent, I fell in love all over again. We were anxious to remove our winter coats and warm clothing, replacing them with airy summer shorts and T-shirts. Socks and tennis shoes were put away to hibernate, while flip-flops would be the only thing gracing our feet at least for the next seven days. We grabbed the camera and headed out toward the beach. There was just so much to see.

Everyone looked six shades tanner here compared to people in Nebraska. I realized that it was wise for Ted to have gone tanning before coming here. It took about five minutes to get to the beach. I was in awe of the miles of blue and green water before me, the white sands that complemented it on the shore, and the many grand hotels at the beach front—all in different shades of pink, blue, and green.

Families were playing in the water. Perfectly toned boys played a game of beach volleyball. With this sight, I was thankful that Ted and I were in terrific shape. When I had first met him, his body had impressed me the most. Even being nine years older, his body was chiseled from the many hours of working construction and roofing. Mine was not bad, either. My size-zero frame was accentuated by my C-cup breasts. We both looked good, and we both knew it. We walked on the beach, then took a little tour of Waikiki.

It had been years since I had gone on anything that resembled a vacation. On school holidays back in Zimbabwe, we had vacationed in places like the mighty Victoria Falls, Kariba, and Mutare. What was best about these trips was that my aunt and uncle, Ann and Simon, who were particular favorites, always came with us.

Ted gasped at every little thing we saw. I believe this was the first vacation Ted had ever been on.

While we strolled the streets of Waikiki, the expression on Ted's face was that of a child experiencing something new and delicious for the first time. He was totally and completely happy.

I was happy, too.

Ted's mother had been married five times. He had seven siblings—five brothers and two sisters, of which he was the youngest boy. After he was born, his mother had put him in the care of her parents at their farm in Onawa, Iowa, in order to pursue a new relationship. He was with his grandparents till the age of three, after which his mother took him back. He had never met his biological father, but he had spoken to him once on the phone. Then, when Ted was fourteen, his father was run over by a car in Las Vegas.

I had met members of his family: his mother, Sally, and her husband Lloyd; his sister Ritter, who was always pregnant, each time I saw her; his other sister, Syd, who, Ted had whispered in my ear when I first met her, "is gay." Syd had two little girls, and she was gorgeous. I had noticed her. His older brother Frank, with whom he shared a father, was in prison for aggravated assault. Another brother was in the army and didn't care much to keep in touch with any of them. One brother lived across his mother's farm, but he had not spoken to any of the family members in years. One other brother was a biker, well into his fifties.

From the time I met his family, it was clear to me that it was a rather dysfunctional one, even by Ted's own admission. He had spent years resenting his mother for his upbringing, how poor he was, and how cruel she had been to him as a child. Ted was the only one in his family who had attempted to go to college, even though he dropped out before graduating.

In a way, both Ted and I had suffered in our childhood. He had felt just as much an outsider as a child in his family as I had in mine. Even though his mother was still living, she had abandoned him right after he was born in order for his grandparents to raise him. We both had never had a relationship with our biological fathers. We had both grown up feeling unloved as children.

I think more than anything it was this childhood pain that connected us. There was something about trying to mend the broken children that were inside us that brought us together. We had both suffered emotionally as children; we both had not ever sought help for that emotional suffering. Deep down in our cores, we were these two wounded souls, desperately trying to navigate and survive in a world that hadn't always been good and fair to us. This was our mutual upbringing, even though we came from completely different parts of the world.

On our second day in Hawaii, a shuttle bus took us to a building, where we had a welcome brunch and the opportunity to sign up for all the adventures and events we wished to partake in during our stay in Oahu Waikiki. Of course, the first thing we signed up for was a luau that very night. For January 17, my twenty-fourth birthday, we signed up for a dinner cruise on the second level of the ship, which would not be the cheapest, but also not the most expensive. We signed up for parasailing for the fifth day, then for a submarine adventure. We were seeking fun.

After having dinner at the TGI Fridays in our hotel, we noticed how expensive everything was in this city. A gallon of milk alone was nearly $5, compared to $1.50 back in Omaha. The gas prices were also way high, which made us happy we had not decided to rent a vehicle. Instead, we would depend on shuttle services. Since this was a tourist town, it wouldn't be a problem.

When brunch was finished, we went down to the beach. The water was much colder than it appeared, and this area had jagged rocks, which made it uncomfortable to walk through the water. After struggling awhile, we were advised to move farther down to warmer waters. Of course, everyone else was down there, which was why we had avoided it in the first place.

I stayed mainly on the shore, while Ted attempted to ride waves with a rented surfboard. I joined him on a water bicycle ride and I gave him the annoying job of asking a stranger every few minutes to take a picture of us. That evening we managed to get a nap in before preparing to be picked up for the luau. We had bought matching shirts in one of the many stands on the streets—red Hawaiian shirts, with big white flowers—so we put those on. I undid a few buttons on the bottom and tied the shirt to reveal my flattened belly and to avoid looking like the old ladies I had seen in matching clothes with their spouses.

The bus we got on was very much alive. A Polynesian man was at the front of the bus, asking everyone to sing after him. We joined in the singing, clapping our hands. He showed us the universal sign for saying hello and good-bye in Hawaiian, putting his three middle fingers against his palm and letting the two outer ones stretch out.

"ALOHA," he emphasized as he twisted his hand, back and forth. Like a chorus, the whole bus repeated after him, "ALOHA." At the end of which, we all laughed and giggled at the silliness of how we sounded in unison.

He told us of the feast that awaited us; the pig that was slowly roasting in the ground; the poi, of which he warned us not to get too excited about, for it didn't taste that great and would probably remind us of a powdery paste of glue. Then there would be the pineapple and the drinks and the dancers.

Our hopes were soaring as we arrived. The place was full of people dressed like us. The atmosphere was very romantic and so freeing. Polynesian sounds filled the air as the waves of the ocean crushed against the shore. We sipped on Blue Hawaii drinks and mai tais, with little Chinese-like umbrellas decorating the cups.

Ted was more affectionate on this night than he had ever been. He held my every gaze, making sure my drink was always full, always having a hand on me—my arm, my thigh, my shoulder.

The pig was finally ready. This was signaled by the blowing of some type of a Polynesian horn. All the tourists abandoned their seats as we ran in the direction of the pit, where the pig was roasting. Two brown-skinned men, with straight black hair cut short, were standing at either end of the pit. Their exposed bodies, except the waist and bikini area, were dripping with sweat from the proximity of the sweltering pit. The main guy chanted some words in a foreign tongue; to which we all clapped, with no idea why we're clapping. The pig was then raised out and taken to the tables, where it was cut up and we all could start serving ourselves.

The show hadn't even begun and I already was saying to myself, *Wow, they sure know how to put on a show!* On the main stage, the fire dancer was putting out flames with his mouth. For some reason, they all had an ability to make sweating look attractive. The girls came on and did the hula dances with such perfection and ease. Ted and I couldn't take our eyes off them.

Again, while watching these women move, I was secretly reminded that there was something about women that moved me. These thoughts were quickly pushed back into their hiding place, where they have resided for so long. As we returned to our hotel, I thought, all people should at least attend one luau in their lifetimes.

    I had been on Depo-Provera since beginning my relationship with Ted. Just a month before our trip, my OB-GYN, Dr. Taggart, had explained how it took some women up to three years after stopping the shot to get pregnant. The earliest you can expect is maybe a year she had convinced me. With this medical knowledge, I had neglected to get my shot when it was due.

    Maybe it was being so far away from home without the hassles of daily life that made us connect so much. Here on this lovely getaway, sex didn't seem like such a chore. My birthday dinner on the ship was wonderful and full of entertainment. I was twenty-four, and at the time it seemed to have been my best birthday yet.

    On about the fifth day, we began having lunch at places like McDonald's, in order to try and save money. In Hawaii, even McDonald's meals came with pineapple. Fast food in Hawaii was also more expensive than anywhere else in the States.

    We went to flea markets, at which we tried to buy a shirt or T-shirt for anyone we could think of. This was the first time since marrying him, I consciously thought about his children. I reminded him to pick something up for them—the two boys in Sioux City, the only ones he could see.

    Shortly after we got married, Ted had tried to contact Zoey. The next thing I knew, he was telling me that he was due in court for disturbing the peace. Apparently, Zoey's parents had pressed charges when he had gone to their house in hopes of seeing his kids. I was upset, as I didn't even know this had occurred until it was close to his court date. He had insisted I go along.

OUTsider

Ted's sentence was six months of probation in which he had to take an anger management class and a parenting class. I had not paid much attention, rationalizing that I, in fact, did not have any children with him and would not be having any for a while. Again I was wrong.

The last few days in Hawaii, we parasailed, which was exhilarating. In the marketplaces, we bought mangos, real mangos, not the ones I was used to buying in Walmart back in Omaha. These were real yellow, sweet, ripe, and juicy mangos like the ones we ate in trees as youngsters in the rural areas of Dzimbadzemabwe (house of stone). That was how the name "Zimbabwe" came about as youngsters.

I also got to taste real sugarcane—not the one in granule form, but real sugarcane, unprocessed with the skin still intact. The peeling was not to be left to a rookie; so with precision, I showed my hubby how it was done. I explained how the edges of the skin were razor sharp and could cut one's mouth open. I watched him try to chew on it in order to extract the juice. It was funny; he had no idea how. It's so amazing how a simple act you grow up doing can be quite a task for someone who has never done it. Ted was better at opening up the oyster shells. I couldn't be bothered with the physical force necessary to crack it open in anticipation of just one pearl, for it wasn't enough to make a necklace.

We explored the nightlife, as it had been one of the reasons we had chosen Waikiki. The other islands were dead by ten, our travel agent had warned. In one bar, we met a bartender named Chief. He was huge, maybe four hundred pounds but muscular. He had never met anyone from Nebraska. Heck, other people from other parts of the country had never heard of Nebraska. Now, to me, that's just plain ignorance. No matter how big or small a state is, shouldn't you at least know it exists? We would meet people and say we're from Nebraska and they would get a puzzled look on their faces.

"And where is that again?" they would often ask.

"You know it's in the Midwest, right in the center of the country."

Still the puzzled look remained.

"Well, have you heard of Iowa?"

"Oh, yeah."

"Well, Nebraska is right next to that."

There is no reason why a grown man or woman in a country where primary and secondary education is free should ever have to learn geography of their own country from a stranger they meet while on vacation!

Bartender Chief told us all about the Polynesian people, a lot about their history, which I didn't know, their rich traditions and culture. On the days we spent sunbathing at the beach, every now and then, a group of Asian tourists would pass by me, stop, and start taking pictures while going on in a very fast language. After about the third time of this happening, I started to wonder what the fascination was with me. I concluded that it was the mere fact that I was black. I had not seen many black people at all since arriving on the island.

I knew there wasn't a big presence of black people in most Asian countries. Ted joked that I was going to end up on some Asian porn website if I kept allowing them to take pictures of me. I really had no say in the matter. They didn't ask for permission. Just from that minor experience, I certainly don't envy celebrities if that happens to them every day. How annoying!

On the day before we were to return to Omaha, we really did not want to leave. So we called the travel agent and for $300 we extended our stay by three more days. I sent postcards to my family back in Omaha, to my aunt and uncle in Zimbabwe, and to a couple of Ted's relatives, too. We had run out of money, but the environment itself was hard to leave. Every time we were at the beach and noticed another homeless person getting into his house made of cardboard box, I often thought that he was probably a tourist who came on vacation and couldn't leave, completely consumed by the beauty to the point of insanity.

The homeless people of Hawaii resembled the homeless people of the capital city of Zimbabwe. Their makeshift homes were close together and their bodies dirty. I must say their presence in this beautiful place, camped along the majestic shores, reminded me that people the world over struggle every day. Even "paradise" is like any place else. The night brought night workers with it—people who would do anything to please a tourist for money.

Sadly, our ten days were up. I would have to return to work. At this rate, if we had stayed another day, we would not have been able to afford even a Happy Meal!

Getting back to six inches of snow after ten days in heat and water was a hard pill to swallow. In the days after arriving, I didn't feel that good. I attributed it to the trip, so I didn't worry. My siblings had had all the time in the world to complain about their harsh, harsh conditions and rules under my care, so it wasn't surprising that their mother was not in a happy mood. Nonetheless, she returned to England.

TWELVE
The Fruits of Paradise

After two weeks of still not feeling okay, I figured surely all the alcohol should be out of my system by now. I had just returned from vacation, where I had done a lot of resting and there was a lot of lovemaking, too.

Could I be pregnant? No way, my doctor had said a year, maybe three years.

Ted and I had talked about having kids and figured by the time a year was up, we would be ready. I decided to buy a home pregnancy test; to my astonishment, it signified that I was pregnant by a pink cross, as opposed to just a line.

My immediate feeling was elation. For the longest time, I had not liked the idea of bringing someone into this world. This thought was shadowed by my early losses and struggles thereafter. The thought of bearing a child and then having something happen to me was terrifying, because that reality of being orphaned had happened to me.

Now, as I looked down at this plastic stick and realized it detected the hormone only present after conception, I felt so at peace. I fell immediately in love with the little girl who was budding inside my womb. Yes, I knew instantaneously it was a girl.

Ted was over the moon with the news and came along when I went to get another confirmation at the doctor's office. It was true, I was indeed expecting. I was already about three weeks or so along. Then it hit me: I was on vacation, drinking like a fish, without realizing I was carrying a baby. I was immediately riddled with guilt. I knew what alcohol did to the unborn. I confessed my fears to my doctor, who didn't seem that concerned. She assured me everything should be fine.

Something about this pregnancy made me very loving toward my husband and my siblings . . . and my adoptive mother not so much. I began to fight with her over the children. She didn't like my rules, but she was very happy with the news of the coming baby. It had been over a year after our wedding. If I had been back home, people would have started talking about my possible infertility by now.

I was the happiest I could ever be, knowing that I was going to bring a life into this world, even with the planet's ugliness. I would make certain I protected this little person I was carrying at all cost. Almost right away, I started to write my baby letters. I would later put these in her baby book. As my belly grew, I felt for the first time that someone truly understood me, and that someone was this baby. She would be someone who will always love me, no matter what. She would be directly related to me and share my blood.

I would have someone whom no one else could ever take away from me.

I created memories for my baby: the date of the first heart sound. Hearing a beating heart within you that's separate from yours was an unbelievable experience, only topped by then seeing an ultrasound picture of moving limbs and the cutest big head you've ever seen. All these things I put in a book with beautiful decorations and the emotions I was feeling at the time. I would write endless letters to my child telling her about who I was, telling her about the love I had for her, promising never to leave, promising always to love with all of me.

I wrote all the things I had longed as a child to hear from my own mother. I explained all the features I longed to remember about my own mother. I described all the characteristics I wish I had known my own mother to possess. I told her about my loud voice and infectious laugh. I told her about the power of fearlessness and the strength of kindness. When I held that pen and watched the formation of my belly, I poured my heart out on paper, until I was spent.

My belly was so toned that it remained almost flat for the longest time. Then, after about the sixth month, I felt this sharp pain. I looked down and saw a footprint. I could clearly count the toes almost protruding out of me, held back by the band of muscle and elasticity of my skin. This little girl was really trying to stretch out.

    At the twenty-week ultrasound, my instincts had been confirmed that I was having a little girl. Ted worked hard, wanting to save money so he could stay home for a little while after I had to return to work. We also decided to try to purchase a home before the newborn arrived. Since his credit was shot, we had to pay off about $3,000 of my debt. With about two months to go in my pregnancy, Norma decided to move here and settle down for Tapiwa and Tashinga's sake. With my grandmother gone and the political unrest, the economy crumbling, there was no reason to stay in Zimbabwe. Norma completed her degree in England and returned once again, this time hoping to stay. She brought Nyasha along, which at the time I thought was a mistake.

THIRTEEN
The Happiest Day of My Life

On September 27, 2004, Chidochemoyo (my heart's desire) was born at 3:39 in the afternoon. She weighed 6.5 pounds, and was 20½ inches in length. I had arrived at the hospital the night before, only to be returned home. Even though my contractions were very painful, they were not close enough together yet.

At about one-thirty in the morning, I had failed to sleep due to the pain of each hard-hitting, belly-tightening contraction. When one would come, I'd freeze and my stomach would become rock hard. The pain was at times shooting. It would stab at me; then there would be a pulsating throb or a burning sensation. Every way there was to describe pain, I experienced it with each coming contraction.

The hospital bag had been ready for months now, filled with pretty pink baby outfits. We had spent the last two months getting her room ready. Norma had moved the kids to a different apartment so our new baby would have her own room. The baby furniture was top of the line. Everything was matching, and her little closet was full of clothes.

I told Ted we needed to go and he tried to help me, but his efforts irked me. I just wanted to get to the hospital. Upon arrival, I was assigned a room and a nurse came in and instructed me to get undressed and put on a hospital gown. I lay down on the bed. She instructed me to part my legs so she could check if I have dilated any.

This took me back to the time I had my first Pap smear exam, after they had insisted I couldn't get on the Depo without one. Who on God's green earth ever invented that kind of torture? Lucky for me, my doctor was gentle and looked like Hilary Swank, with a perfect smile that put me at total ease. How did women ever allow male doctors to perform this act on them? When choosing an OB-GYN, I made a conscious choice to have it be a female. I would have never been comfortable with a male doctor. I just had an internal chasm regarding men and my private parts. I preferred to have the two separate.

It was a relief that all the nurses happened to be female as well.

"One centimeter," the nurse said as she stood and swiftly tried to remove the bloody-looking glove from her right hand with her left. She informed me that she'd put a call out to Dr. Taggart and return to me.

Ted remained at my side, offering words of comfort when my face turned into agony. When the nurse returned with news that I could get an epidural as soon as my liter of IV fluid was up, I was so glad. When asked if I wanted an epidural for pain, there was no hesitation at all. I wasn't trying to be anyone's hero and had researched and discovered that there were very little effects to the new baby, despite what many women believed.

Trying to sit up with my shoulders curved so as to arch my back for the anesthesiologist to gain easy entry into my spine was a difficult task with the contractions now coming every other minute. My nurse, Julie, was very patient and sweet. She held my hand and Ted stood looking on. After the first sting of the numbing needle, I felt no other pain. In five minutes' time, almost like magic, I could not feel a thing. I still felt my stomach tighten, but the pain that had come with it was completely gone. My legs turned into jelly and I needed help to raise them up when necessary.

The following morning, Norma came to the hospital to be with us. Before this, I had never actually imagined having my adoptive mother and my husband in the same room while my genital area was in open view for all to see. That's the beauty of life; because at that present moment, it didn't seem weird at all. It actually seemed natural.

My doctor had stopped by the previous night and suggested that if the dilation was not going well by seven the next morning, then she would order Pitocin to be run to speed up the process. With the Pitocin coursing through my veins, and the epidural infusing into my spinal fluid,

I was feeling good. I had managed to sleep free of pain. I was feeling so good that I started making calls to friends and family on my cell phone, shocking them with the news that I could give birth at any moment. "So how can you be talking" was the response I got. That's the beauty of pain medication—what a great invention!

After two o'clock in the afternoon, the nurse explained that we were almost there: "Eight centimeters, but only fifty percent effaced." She placed a call to my doctor and Dr. Taggart arrived at approximately three o'clock. After getting draped in the proper attire, complete with mask and goggles, she went to work. She had to play around with an area of scar tissue, she said, while down there. It must have been from the time I received a cryotherapy procedure to remove possible cancerous tissue from the opening of my cervix.

Dr. Taggart had performed it, advising that even though it was not cancerous now, it could potentially develop into such. This procedure would take care of it once and for all. The day I had the procedure done, it had left me sick to my stomach with a dizzying pain. After a few days, I was back to normal, content with the knowledge that cervical cancer would not ever victimize me. After the palpation of the scar tissue, my effacement was complete within minutes.

Now dilated to ten centimeters, the pushing could begin. My adoptive mother and husband stood at either side of my legs, looking on with such excitement in their eyes.

"She has lots of hair," someone said.

"Oh, it looks like I have to cut you, just a little," Dr. Taggart said; and within seconds, my firstborn daughter announced her entry into the world with a high-pitched cry.

I was overcome with emotion just at the sound of her cry. Tears of joy were overflowing. In that instant, this gaping void that I had carried within my heart for so long was closed. A new sense of self came over me—a happiness I had never before experienced—almost as if every little thing I had endured in my life had led me to this very moment. If I was never meant for anything else in this world, maybe—just maybe—I was only meant for this, to be the mother of this beautiful little girl.

After Ted helped cut the umbilical cord, my baby was placed on my chest. She was much longer than I expected, and she had the cutest chubby cheeks, plump red lips, and huge eyes. Her complexion couldn't be more opposite mine. She was a very rosy pink and the black short hairs on her head were straight. With ten fingers and ten toes, she was perfect.

We're congratulated by all the staff, and I noticed a tear falling down Ted's face as he admired his new little girl lying quietly in the warmer. I said a silent prayer, thanking God for this blessing, the smoothness of the delivery, and for making this the best day of my life.

FOURTEEN
A Baby Works Magic

On the third day, we left the hospital. Our little princess was all buckled up in her brand-new car seat. She had started drinking Enfamil Formula from birth in the hospital. I had decided not to breast-feed, which Norma felt was an atrocity. I had done my research, however, and found the differences between breast and formula feeding to be trivial. Besides, if Ted was going to be an equal partner in this and stay home after I returned to work, formula was the best way to go.

Fellow Zimbabweans came to our apartment to congratulate and marvel at our new beauty. My friend Jenny had visited me in the hospital. After telling her to find the baby in the nursery, she had returned to the room a little worried, explaining that all the infants in the nursery were white babies. We all laughed because clearly Ted's genes had defeated mine, so it seemed. In the days after she was born, her eyes were a shade of blue, eventually taking to their true color of a gorgeous light brown, unlike my dark brown or her father's true blue.

Having a baby in the house changed everything. We automatically became better people, seldom getting angry with each other, working together as a team, taking nightly turns to wake up and feed the baby as necessary. She always ended up sleeping on either one of our chests, never using the expensive crib in her room. We never put her down, either. One of us was holding her at all times, even while she slept.

Two weeks after her birth, we moved into our new home in La Vista. We wanted our child to grow up with a backyard to play in and a place she could call her own. The house had been Ted's choice; I would have preferred a newer home. Since he was coming up with the $7,000 needed for a down payment on the purchase, I couldn't argue much. We used a U-Haul and in less than three days we had managed to move into our new home. Upon purchase, both of our names appeared on the deed of the house, but only my name was on the loan, due to Ted's bad credit and back child support.

After six weeks of maternity leave, I returned to work at the nursing home, where I now worked in the Health Information Management Office. Getting this position was a relief, especially throughout my pregnancy. It saved my back and feet, for I sat at a desk all day inputting physicians' orders and care plans. I had worked the floor for four years doing much physical work, which I didn't mind, as I enjoyed interacting with the residents. The residents' families easily took a liking to me, and I can honestly say, I did my work to the best of my ability and with a caring heart.

Leaving my "Honey Girl" home on that first day back to work was hard. She was awake and her dad was holding her. As I kissed her good-bye, she let out a cry as if she knew I was going. The whole drive to work, I wiped away tears, feeling like I was abandoning her somehow. In the month that he stayed home with her after I returned to work, Ted was really good about bringing the baby to work at lunchtime so I could see her. Then he would spend another half hour showing her off. My Chido, my baby sister's namesake, looked just like the "Gerber Baby." Everywhere we went, people would stop us and want to see her closer. She was very aware and always opened her eyes in a great big way. She always smiled and was never fussy.

FIFTEEN
Bad Behavior Comes to Call

Ted soon returned to his meat salesman job, which he had begun after his business partner had disappeared after being wanted by the police. He made decent money selling meat door-to-door, but Ted simply had no knowledge of financial stability. He began buying cars at auctions and selling them. He started collecting car parts and buying old run-down cars, like a 1954 Chevy, in the hopes of restoring it one day. He was a real hoarder. He would keep any piece of junk he ever came across, and soon there was just no space in our new home.

Since we now had a house, on some weekends he brought his two boys from Sioux City to spend the weekend. Now being a parent myself, I had become more accommodating. I was starting to encourage him to be a better father, not just to our child but to all his offspring.

While looking through his stuff, back when we were at the apartment, I had discovered a wedding photo album in which Ted was clearly the groom and some red-haired white woman was the bride. There were also pictures of a little girl, who possessed his smile. Only then did he admit to having been married previously and he went on to explain how Zoey, his ex with the two kids in Omaha, had encouraged him to sign away parental rights to the little girl, so he wouldn't have to deal with child support.

I was frustrated with the unending tales of his past. How fertile could one guy be? Also, all these kids were very close in age. I was married to him now, so what was there to do but to deal with it?

In the few instances that I ever brought up his past to his mother, she had always called his exes "bitches" and had always blamed them for wronging her son. Ted worked mostly out of town during the week and would return on Fridays. He would then spend the weekend working on a car or two. His cars started to consume most of his free time. When something was not working right with the cars, I would hear him throw a part while screaming obscenities at objects that couldn't hear. My concern, though, was for the neighbors who could.

Ted definitely had a short temper. Our new baby, whom he called "Lover Girl," had mellowed him down a little bit. Still, it would always creep up out of him, almost unforeseen. I remember an incident during the first few weeks of being in our new home. We had argued about something related to his other two boys, who were with us for the weekend. In his rage, Ted had flipped the glass coffee table in our living room in the direction I sat with our newborn daughter. Luckily, it had not broken, but I was so shaken by this. I could not believe what he had just done. Then, like usual, he had cried a river and apologized.

We spent the rest of that day with my aunt Norma and my siblings at the zoo. He and I walked around holding hands, like nothing violent had ever transpired. I had accepted his abusive nature as a normal part of our relationship.

SIXTEEN
Lightning Strikes Twice

Being a mother made me want to make something out of my life. I decided to obtain a nursing degree. I started taking the necessary prerequisites at Metropolitan Community College, where I had been previously enrolled. For my English composition class, I submitted a fifteen-page research paper on "Why America Needs Universal Health Care." Stating reasons such as it was the only industrialized nation without Universal Health Care, using video footage from Michael Moore's preview of his documentary *Sicko* to illustrate facts, giving examples from my own personal life when I had lived briefly in the United Kingdom, I delivered my project to the class. The problem, I had said to my classmates, was that Americans in general are very frightened to try new things and explore different ways of doing things.

Giving birth here in the United States, I had been lucky to have health care insurance through my job. Without employment, I wouldn't have had coverage. Plus, even with my health insurance, I still received a bill of more than $3,000 after my daughter was born to pay as an out-of-pocket expense. After a heated debate, I had put my point across and received applause as I took my seat.

In my anatomy and physiology class, I had stunned everyone with the revelation that between 1932 and 1972 the U.S. Public Health Service conducted a study to monitor the natural progression of untreated syphilis in rural African-American men who resided in Tuskegee, Alabama. These black men had previously contracted syphilis and were misled to believe they were receiving free health care from the government.

I was equally as stunned to know that out of a full classroom of adults, the teacher was the only other person aware of this fact. This teacher came to my rescue when others became angry with what I had said.

I will never forget a comment one woman had made about me to someone else, "How does a person from Africa know so much?"

In my mind, in retaliation, I thought, *How does a person from America know so little?*

Shortly after Chido was born, Aunt Norma would come to me with suspicions that Nyasha was possibly pregnant. Her suspicions were raised by Nyasha's continual weight gain since they arrived five months prior. I told Norma I would buy a home pregnancy test and would see if Nyasha would agree to take it.

When they arrived at my house, Nyasha completely denied the allegations, even swearing on my grandmother's grave. When the results came back as positive, she still denied it, saying there had to be some big mistake. Luckily, the pack I had bought had a second test, which proved, again, she was to be a mother.

Aunt Norma sobbed bitterly at the news. I was saddened, too, not because of her young age and unwed status. She was six years my junior and had admitted to us that the only possible father of her child was Phillip, a prominent businessman in Zimbabwe, close to her own father's age, if not older. He was like the Donald Trump of Zimbabwe in terms of his wealth. In terms of his character, he was simply the scum of the earth, preying on young girls like my sister with his money and charm.

Nyasha was only eighteen and already six months along with this filthy man's child. When had he started sleeping with her was my only concern—anyone and everyone who is Zimbabwean knows of his many women and children. With AIDS running rampant in our home country, I feared the worst, not only for Nyasha but for her unborn child.

Nyasha began seeing a doctor immediately; and just before Chido turned five months old, Andre was born. I was in the room when he arrived, looking plump like a king. It was surreal. His birth made me realize that no matter what, the circumstance surrounding our conception as human beings, when we arrive, we're all special and created for a very good reason. Andre was soon Chido's best friend.

The biggest fight I've ever had with my aunt Norma was over Andre's father. I guess Nyasha's mother had forgiven him for what he had done and seemed hopeful for his and Nyasha's relationship to continue. This made me furious.

My adoptive mother suggested I learn to forgive, but there was no way I could see this foe as a friend. I loved Andre, but I'll never give an ounce of respect to the man named Phillip. It is because of men like him that African girls are victimized and undervalued. It is because of men like him, in a society where money is in short fall, they're idolized, even when they commit the most heinous acts. My aunt Norma's idolization for this man made me enraged and red with anger, to the point of almost fistfighting her to prove my point. At last, I called the police, lest my anger got the best of me.

After this heated argument, it would take months to communicate with Norma and my cousin-siblings again. I cut them off, deciding to end contact after another incident in which Nyasha had told me to my face that it wasn't *her fault* that my biological mother committed suicide. This was honestly such a low blow! I have no idea why she was bringing my mother's suicide into this—perhaps to prove to me that I wasn't her mother's child? However, her mentioning my mother's suicide was the absolute last straw. I was done with them all.

Surprisingly, it was Nyasha who would hunt me down, trying to call me after months, sobbing through the phone as she told me of how she suspected that Norma might be sick and possibly close to death, but was keeping it from everyone. There had been things I had noticed about Norma that I had questioned, and all Nyasha was now telling me made sense. I wept so much that day, thinking I had gone so long without talking to my *only mother*—a woman who may have needed me in all the months I kept my distance, just over my beliefs and opinions. I picked up the phone that very day and made amends, promising myself that I would not ever let an opinion or belief—no matter how strong—keep me away from my loved ones.

My aunt Norma, who was a mother to me, is alive and well today. I don't think she ever told a soul about whatever it was she overcame. The ways in which I would be thankful for her would come later and be greater than I could comprehend.

My Honey Girl, who had many nicknames, would soon be a one-year-old. How time flew! In that year, Norma and her children had secured permanent residency through filing for asylum. The conditions in Zimbabwe kept getting worse. At this announcement, I realized that I still hadn't processed my change of status.

I now nagged Ted about my need for his birth certificate. He promised to call Onawa, the place he had been born, to locate his birth record. In the different times we had argued about politics and immigration, I would get so offended by his racial, xenophobic, patriotic, conservative, one-sided opinions about how Mexicans took all the jobs and were good for nothing.

How could he be married to a black African and have kids who were all part black, except for one, and talk this way? He had a nephew who was part Mexican. In these moments, I realized that he, too, was just like the white people who on many occasions, and at different places, had stared at us, yelling blasphemy with their piercing looks because we were an interracial couple.

One time, while watching TV, he had expressed his dislike of all the Mexicans causing overpopulation.

I looked at him and said, "I, your wife, am illegal, even as we speak."

"Well, you work and you're going to school. So it's not the same."

"Really?" I said.

This must have scared him some. In the following week, he called around, inquiring about his birth record. He was informed that the only record available for a male born to Sally, on his particular birth date, was one with no first name for the child and the last name of Sonyers. He had explained to me that Browner was a stepfather's last name, but one would at least expect his first name to be on his birth certificate.

I had asked him how he had managed to get anything done if he had never actually had a birth certificate. Apparently, his mother had just explained to anyone who needed to know that his name was Ted Browner—no formal change, no legal document to show this—and this man was already in his mid-thirties.

Of course, he did not have a real, on-the-books job, as his pay would all go to child support. He had worked odd construction jobs most of his young adult life. He spoke to his brother, who had the same problem, and his brother explained that he had to go through a lawyer in order to make his unofficial adopted name an alias. Since the immigration lawyer I had consulted had told me that all would be okay once I submitted the necessary documents, I worried a bit, but not a great deal. After all, I had made it somehow with my current illegal status.

We had Chido's first birthday party at Chuck E. Cheese's and invited lots of family and friends. She received many gifts and a battery-operated pink Barbie Jeep from me and Ted. During the week of our little girl's birthday, I had also found out that I would be a mom for the second time.

A blood test at the doctor's office had confirmed it. But unlike the breeze I had while carrying Chido, this child was of a different breed. Right from the start, I was so sick. Every little smell and taste made me nauseous. There were days I would try to swallow my multivitamin, but then I would throw it up. The pungent regurgitation left a bitter taste all the way up my throat and mouth.

Dr. Taggart initially had me try some over-the-counter antiemetic, as I was losing weight instead of gaining. That effort was fruitless, so she finally prescribed Zofran 4mg QD—mostly used to combat nausea in patients receiving chemotherapy. With the first pill I popped, the drug worked like a charm. I drank the rest of the Gatorade I used to take the pill with; ten minutes afterward, there was nothing, no need to run to the bathroom to throw it back up.

From the heavy nausea symptom alone, which was entirely absent in my first pregnancy, I knew then that this child would be a boy. My mood especially toward Ted was different as well. I had been needy the first time, wanting a lot of his attention, noticing his handsomeness almost every day. With this baby, however, I could not stand Ted; or maybe it was just the weight of being with someone, whom I loved so passionately, but also hated with the same passion, which was starting to wear on me.

The hustle and bustle of having a toddler to constantly run after, work, plus another grown child to care for—I mean, hubby—left me with little energy. Even when I wanted to write something to my unborn child, I didn't write it fast enough, or I didn't have the time. In silent moments, I would talk to my belly, telling my baby how proud I would be of him.

The months moved much quicker this time around. When we did the ultrasound, I was so put off by the lady administering the scan. She questioned me about my fluid intake in a harsh tone; then she asked Ted to ensure that Chido was quiet. He stomped out of the room with his Lover Girl, only to miss the image of our unborn son displaying his manhood, clearly pointing up for the world to see. This image I would need to have and keep, just to show his girlfriends in the teen years, which were sure to come.

With Ted having three sons—one of which I knew was his favorite—I was surprised to see him react with pride at the news of our boy. He almost did a dance! I guess boys just have a way of making their fathers feel proud, even if the dad already has a school of them.

SEVENTEEN
The Happiest Day of My Life . . . Part 2

After delivering Chido, my body and belly had instantly returned back to normal and shape. My coming son stretched me far out with each day, bringing streaks of stretch marks across my belly. I spent countless dollars on creams and lotions, which did little to slow this down. Shopping for a baby boy, after only looking at little girl's clothes, was more exciting than I thought. There were so many cute ways to dress little boys, too.

As his due date of June 26 was approaching, I had become impatient. My son was obviously bigger than my daughter and I had gained a little more weight, too. I was relieved when on June 21, 2006, I started to feel contractions, which I now knew for sure signaled labor. Though initially he had proven impossible, my son's birth went much like my daughter's. It was filled with numbing pain medication, in the same hospital, with the same doctor and some of the same nurses.

I never thought it possible to have two of the best days of my life, but when I saw my son for the first time, the love I felt made me cry. He was such a handsome boy, so content. His beauty was so precious to me that it became his nickname: "Handsome Boy." He hardly made a stir, unlike his big sister. His gogo (grandmother) and aunts and uncles flocked in to see him. His big family from Iowa also came, his grandma and grandpa, cousins and aunts.

It was on the second day that Nyasha would notice that Simba had a speck underneath his left eye, his little paw print birthmark.

As he grew up, I told him that God had taken the most precious of His puppies and had made the puppy touch Simba's face with a paw, which had been dipped in a special ink just for him.

Of course, my son would laugh, saying, "No, He didn't, Mommy"; to which I said, "Of course, He did. I was there."

My Simbarashe (God's strength) was born close to four o'clock, weighing 6 pounds 7 ounces and measuring 21 inches long. We all say men have it easy, but that's only because they have it the hard way as little boys. Seeing my baby son's penis after his circumcision, looking like it had been chopped in half, was scary. It looked like it would never heal. After a week of careful washing and handling after we returned home, it did heal, and my boy would be a clean man.

My decision to allow him to be circumcised, coming from a culture where men weren't, was made easy from the years of working in a nursing home and seeing old men, one at a hundred, having to get circumcised due to recurrent urinary tract infections.

These future old-age ailments seemed a million miles away on the day my Handsome Boy was born. His big sister was brought into the room shortly afterward. I held her baby brother in one arm and her in the other; with her first look at him, she had cried angrily. She seemed to be possessive and jealous that this new person was sharing space that she alone had occupied for less than two years. Soon she would be so happy with her new role of bringing Mommy a diaper for the baby, or helping Mommy hold the bottle for the baby.

The second time around, we had learned our lessons from Chido. So, right off the bat, our "Mr. Babba" was sleeping in his own bed, while Chido was still in our bed. We woke him up less frequently at night, which made it all seem so much easier. The problems we had created for ourselves as new parents now seemed like a joke.

EIGHTEEN
Minor Children and Major Changes

As he grew, my son's eagerness with food could be seen in his chubby little frame. Unlike our princess, this guy didn't play when it came to eating. He wanted, and he wanted it all! He urged us to feed him, without any breaks between bites, just ignoring the act of chewing altogether. He scarfed down his baby food at an amazing speed. By two, Chido was potty training, which was a much-needed relief, especially for our budget. Buying diapers for two babies at once was expensive.

I had finally completed my prerequisites for the nursing program before my son was born. I was ecstatic upon getting the official letter congratulating me for being admitted into the LPN program. Due to the high volume of applicants at this community college, to have had the grades good enough and a GPA high enough to be one of the seventy-five admits was huge, especially on a first try. When my baby boy was only three months old, I began nursing school. I returned to work part-time and gave up my position in the office, as it needed a full-time employee.

The few years I had spent in the office, sharing space with Tami, Daphne, Denise, and one of the smartest women I ever met, Sherry, had been so pleasant. From Sherry, I had learned silently that one is never too old for school, and that going to school never has to stop. Because with her master's degrees, her quest for knowledge never ceased. Sherry was always taking some class.

Kathy was my first nursing instructor. She was getting up there in age, but she was young at heart and had a rather reckless spirit. I much enjoyed her teaching style, even though many had a lot to complain about.

My very first test in nursing school I missed one question and scored 98, making it the highest score in the class, which quickly gave me a boost and an unwanted reputation. Nursing school challenged me in ways I welcomed. Ted had to step up to the plate, not just by working harder to pay the bills, but also by taking care of the children on the weekend when he was home and I had to be at the library studying for a test or catching up on notes.

The clinical experiences in the hospitals and nursing homes were unforgettable. Our initial exposure was being on a floor for patients on ventilators—both young and old. Some were here as a result of recklessness; some were rendered ill by the inheritance of a genetic disease, like cystic fibrosis. The patients close to my own age were the hardest to care for emotionally, as it was hard not to picture them able to do daily activities we all take for granted, like standing up. In this rotation, we quickly learned that in order to be a nurse one had to possess true compassion, for it took more than brains to give such care.

Ted complained at times, mainly because my excuses to avoid intimacy at all cost became even worse during this first year of nursing school. Now, on top of the regular, constant headache and the period, there was also exhaustion from schoolwork and a test to study for after the kids had gone to sleep. He had a vasectomy, which he had agreed to two months after our son was born. His total was now seven children. Ted had tried to claim that one of his sons was not biologically his, which led the mother to get DNA results. The DNA test proved that he had, in fact, fathered that child. Ted thought somehow that because he had no part in more than half his children's lives, they didn't exist.

I made sure to go with him to the urologist's office the day of the procedure, knowing it was the most canceled surgery. I had to make sure he would not chicken out. After he had waddled to the car, not wanting his freshly cut scrotum to touch his clothing, he was sad, a tear coming out of just one eye.

"What's the matter?" I asked.

"No more little Teds. . . ." He actually sobbed.

I don't think if he had the job of carrying the pregnancies of all the children he had fathered, he would be sitting there crying because he was no longer fertile. I think he would be rejoicing, like I was.

Whenever I brought up the issue, he would say things like, "Those aren't my kids, anyways. I don't even get to see them."

I couldn't help but see him as a tall, dark man like my father was, standing there denying me in the presence of some woman. Once you conceive a child, that child is yours—no matter how far they go, no matter your presence in their life, no matter the legal documents, giving and taking away rights. The genetic code of a parent can never be altered or erased.

Later on, Ted's new girlfriend would call me "Africa" to my face. She would tell my only son that she was his mother and I would be getting deported back to Africa, where I belonged.

I would look at her and say, "My son will always be my son."

I often wondered how Ted managed to go on every day, knowing he had three children who lived in the same city—his two boys and one girl, who were born and raised by their mothers in Sioux City, Iowa—but he had no part in their lives, not in the slightest of ways. During our first year, he had shed a tear on his two kids' birthdays—the ones in Omaha—and he had talked about missing the way they were growing up. I had urged him to try to contact them in some way, but after the probation sentence he did not want to risk another violation.

I knew that our two children and I made him very happy and completed his world, but I often felt like we were rugs, which he used to cover a big hole in the ground. With one wrong push or move, the rug could at any time fall inward, revealing the gaping hole that it concealed.

NINETEEN
A Black-and-White Issue

In one of my clinical experiences in nursing school, I experienced racism that rocked my core and made me realize for the first time why some African Americans feel so strongly about it. Sure, I had run into the occasional old lady at Good Sam who had said she didn't want a black person as her attendant; but with these old folks, after a while of getting used to you, they no longer felt that way.

On the day of the clinical, I had arrived on the floor at Midlands and had received a report that said the man to be my patient was at times hard to care for. Confident in my communication skills, as well as my nursing skills, I walked into the room with all the necessary equipment to collect my patient's morning vitals. I had a stethoscope around my neck; I was pulling the electronic blood pressure cuff behind me. I grabbed the thermometer hanging on the wall as I entered the room.

My warm hello and self-introduction of "Hello, sir, my name is Ruth and I am a student nurse with Metro Community College, and I will be your nurse today" was not reciprocated.

As I proceeded to extend a hand, so as to gauge on his upper arm where to place the cuff to record his blood pressure, he harshly said, "Don't touch me!"

I stepped back and said, "I need to take your morning vitals, sir, if that's okay."

"No, it's not okay. I want my regular nurse to do it. I don't want someone like you touching me."

This man was maybe in his mid-forties, so he was not an old-timer like the ones I had forgiven for such words. He was overweight and unhygienic. It blew my mind that in his conceited thoughts, he felt he would be doing me some kind of favor by allowing me to do my work, which entailed me putting my black hands on his "precious" white skin.

I calmly left his room in search of my instructor, thinking I could brush it off, get a new patient, and my day wouldn't be wasted. When I related to my teacher that I wanted a new patient, she became defensive. I explained what just happened, and she became even more defensive, suggesting that I take another nurse in with me. For some reason, I was ashamed just to say he was a racist.

She brought yet another nurse to me who also tried to convince me that this man who had treated me that way was just mean, but not irrational; I could somehow talk him into nicely letting me take care of him. I felt myself start to shake. For the first time, I wished there were another person of my race in my clinical group or on the staff working on that floor. Someone who could maybe understand what I was trying to get across.

In that instant, it all seemed so unfair: being the only black person here, having only a few black people in the nursing program at a community college in the center of a black neighborhood. Why were we so few? The few being African and the real people intended for this affordable college. Why were low-income African Americans hardly represented?

As my head rushed with thoughts of discrimination and lack of understanding, I started to cry and walked away so as not to cause a scene. My instructor followed, finally recognizing the seriousness of the matter. She quickly apologized, not knowing what to do.

I was embarrassed that I let my emotions get the best of me. I was supposed to be professional.

"Sometimes things hurt, in ways we can't control" was what I told my classmates, who would later approach me, one by one, secretly trying to get a piece of the main story from the gossip column of the day.

Or maybe they actually did care and felt as helpless as I did?

TWENTY
Saving Others, but Not Myself

The experiences I gained on my clinical rotations of my first year were mostly positive and exciting, like witnessing a precipitous delivery in which the nurses, me included, had to deliver the baby without the doctor's presence. Babies don't wait to make sure everyone who is supposed to be there is there before they decide to come out. I learned baffling facts, like most women refuse to get HIV tested during their pregnancies.

Academically, nursing school was grueling and tough. Many students failed quarterly tests and flunked out; some students had only one quarter to go. We had to become familiar with almost all disease processes, had to be familiar with drug names and uses for pharmacology, and everything that had to do with health and wellness.

Out of the classroom, my nursing skills were really tested one day while dining at an Applebee's with my family—the very same one that Ted and I had met in after he had stood me up. At the table behind us, a child started coughing nonstop. From the sound he made, it was clearly airway obstruction.

His young mother looked across to her own mother, saying, "He's choking, Mom! He's choking!"

His grandmother couldn't seem to move; she remained seated across from where the little boy sat.

Unconsciously, I found myself at their table, pulling the boy out of his high chair, which was not very efficient in an emergency scenario like this one. I put him facedown on my lap and gave him two strong thuds on his back, while holding his chin with my other hand underneath him. A cheesy piece of macaroni, non-masticated, was propelled four feet or so away. The coughing stopped and the ruby-red color started to disappear from his face. He even let out a smile, somewhat amused, unfazed by what had occurred. He must have been about my son Simba's age, eight months or so.

The mother and grandmother thanked me; the diners around applauded. I returned to my seat, only after offering the mother further instructions on what to do if it ever occurred again.

Ted was genuinely proud, saying, "At least our money is going to good use."

That was the most heroic action I have ever taken; and without my nursing knowledge, I never would have summoned up the courage to do it.

TWENTY-ONE
The Past Crosses My Path

I graduated with a certificate as a licensed practical nurse in May 2007; the achievement felt minute as I was now eager to become an RN, even before I had taken my boards. LPN boards were a walk in the park, because not only did I pass, but so did everyone else. I mean, all sixty-five of us who had managed to complete the program passed on our very first try. I guess a first for a group that large in Omaha.

That June, my son turned one. It felt amazing to be able to have his birthday party right in our own backyard, with the warm weather introducing the beginning of summer. Kids chased one another around, while grown-ups feasted on grilled sausages and pork chops. We were the epitome of a true all-American family.

I'm sure most of the Zimbabweans who brought their kids must have looked at us with envy. They must have thought me so lucky to be married to this handsome white man and have such beautiful kids. I couldn't recall how it had happened so quickly: my son's first year of life, but my days literally just spun dealing with school, work, and kids. Plus, I was all alone with them during the week, while Ted was on the road selling meat. When he would return home on the weekends, some car always needed tending. I felt like a single parent and was learning to be okay with it.

I knew Ted loved our kids very much. He showed it in the nicknames he had for them, in the way he held them and kissed them and told them he loved them. I just wished he loved them enough to stop cussing and being angry at the world all the time. Since I met him, Ted always walked around like each and every person he came across had wronged him in some way. He never cared about being polite with strangers or neighbors. A receptionist at work once asked me after answering his call, "Why is he so angry all the time?" It was as if the only way he could get respect was by being aggressive. He felt the need always to put up a fight, even when it was uncalled for.

Initially I had thought no one had really given him a chance, no one had really loved him enough. He had even told me that if only I loved him enough, then he wouldn't be so angry—that would be all he needed.

If you cannot find happiness within yourself, nobody can ever make you happy. This was something I had learned over time, even when I had been just a little girl.

August came around bringing a new round of nursing school. The RN program would prove to be much more challenging than the last. It would also bring about an unplanned connection with someone from Ted's past.

In September, Chido turned three. We celebrated that birthday at the Bounce U. One day, while at the Fort Omaha Campus, a week or so before my RN program was about to begin, I was sitting outside the library on a bench. Suddenly I looked up, and a face I had seen many years before passed by. Some faces you just never forget.

As soon as she disappeared behind the doors of the nursing offices, I got up to look at the new list of teachers for the nursing program. The list confirmed my suspicions. Indeed, Zoey was now a new nursing instructor at the school.

I told myself to relax and not panic much, for it didn't mean she would be teaching me, right? Wrong. I soon found out that indeed Ted's ex fiancée, with whom he had children, whom he had not seen in almost five years, was to be one of my instructors for the next three quarters.

The first thing I did was tell Ted. He seemed unaffected, reiterating again what a bitch she was. After being called this myself by the same person so many times in our relationship, I didn't side with him on this opinion. I decided, instead, to see if there was a way I could maybe clear the air with her before classes started, thereby avoiding an awkward situation.

I got her cell phone number from one of the other students who had been in her clinical group, explaining to them my need to dispel any differences or emotional tensions. After gathering up some courage, I dialed the number, a little tremulous, not sure why I should be nervous.

She answered and I said, "Hello. Uh, hi! Yeah, this is Ruth and I am Ted's wife. I'm not sure if you remember me, but I met you a long time ago when you brought your kids over to Ted's apartment."

I waited for a response, which was that she simply didn't remember who I was.

I said, "Okay. Well, the reason I'm calling is to clear the air with you. I just don't want it to be an awkward situation in the classroom. I realize yours and Ted's past is a bad one, but I'm hoping that we can work as professionals."

She responded by telling me about her list of degrees, including a master's, and concluded by saying that she obviously would be professional.

I said "thank you"; but before she hung up, she offered an invitation to her office for an introduction whenever I was at school next. I was satisfied with the conversation, glad it had gone the way I hoped.

The next Tuesday, I had class. I went up to her office, looking a little dressier than usual. I guess trying not to look like her ex's trashy wife. As I entered her office, my attention focused on the wall. In an 8 x 10 photo frame, the little blond boy I had seen before had indeed added five years to his body and face. He looked very handsome, with dimples unmistakably belonging to his father. His hair was cut very short; and next to him sat his little sisters. One, the older of the two girls, could easily have been Chido's sister. Another one, a new addition, looked like her sister in the picture, she was Zoey's child with her new husband.

Zoey initiated small talk, but I couldn't hear what she said. In that moment, my thoughts went to Ted, wishing he were there, standing in my place, looking at these beautiful children he had created.

I had to give it to him. If there was one thing he did well, it was make good-looking kids. Every single one of his seven kids was overtly beautiful. I called Ted later in the day and told him about how beautiful his children were and how much they had grown. He was excited about this news, but his voice broke, a little overcome with emotion.

TWENTY-TWO
His Ex Marks the Spot

After a while, I started to think that this coincidence was supposed to help Ted reconnect with his children somehow. I talked to him about maybe writing a letter. No, in fact, I wrote a letter for him stating how sorry he was for the many years of absence from the kids' lives and how he was such a better man now—with a wife, kids, and a home. If there was any way he could make things right, as far as the kids were concerned, he would. We read the letter and proofread it again before sending it via e-mail to an address we Googled on the Internet, wanting to avoid her school in-box.

Ted received a letter back from her via the post office with no return address. It simply stated how good the kids were, and how little they remembered of him. The boy recalled more than the girl, but all that he remembered was bad. Zoey wrote that they had a caring father now, one who took them to soccer practice and ballet lessons, one who was present on sick nights. She concluded with the introduction of her new daughter and by saying that he could not come into their lives now. It would be too disruptive. She had not planned on telling her kids about him until they were much older.

I assume that on his way to sell meat during that week, alone in his van, that he must have cried. He must have felt bad for not having been a better man. My attempt to collect maybe just a photo of his kids for him failed. Zoey absolutely refused to give him even a photograph.

Then the stories started floating in the class. Some told me of how she said her ex had abused her so much, punching her while she was pregnant. I became so defensive when I heard this, denying the allegations on his behalf, singing his praises, and calling her crazy. Deep down inside, I knew that what she said was neither fiction nor exaggeration. It would not be far-fetched for Ted to have done those things. He had done them to me and to everyone else before me.

How does one man father seven kids with four different women in a space of ten or so years? Had we all been so irrational? Had we all used him for his good looks, just for our benefit, so we could then have these amazing-looking children, then discard him like a used rag? That was certainly the picture he had painted when coloring the demise of all his prior relationships when I had demanded an explanation. In the not-so-distant future, I, too, would be added to this list of those who had apparently used him.

When my attempts failed to arrange a happy reunion for a long-lost father and his children, I decided to take my hands out of it and focus, instead, on the thing I was there to do in the first place: my school work. I respected Zoey's teaching. I found her to be knowledgeable and honest regarding the questions she had no answers to. She and another teacher accused my friend Carol of looking at my test answers during one test. When I was questioned by the director of nursing, whom I also had tremendous respect for, I told her it was highly unlikely. I then wondered if Zoey had an agenda, after all. Carol's much higher grade and the difference in her wrong answers, compared to mine, proved the allegations false—a fact I was sure to make certain the Department of Nursing had not missed. We were, however, very careful after that, lest our eyes wander and be taken for spying again. Our friend Rachel agreed to sit between us.

As the year progressed, having this blast from the past made me really evaluate my life, my marriage, and my goals. Zoey had found a way to sever the ties to the person she knew held her back. Was it possible that I could do the same? Could I find the courage within to somehow confront the monster and admit unhappiness?

I hinted that Ted needed help with his anger. I suggested therapy, and said I would even go with him. I had been asking Ted to change since the first incident on the basketball court many years back when we first met. He had never done so—marrying me and having our beautiful children had not removed his anger. We had not made him happy, like I had hoped.

Like any other time when I had brought up his anger issues and how it affected the kids, he would be well behaved, for a week maybe two. Catching himself before letting a four-letter word slip out of his mouth in our midst, apologizing for the near mishap. Then, like clockwork, something would happen that would tick him off so much that no amount of restraint in the world could prevent him from blowing up into a raging maniac, as if crippled with a form of extended Tourette's syndrome. Ted could not stop his anger, no matter how much he tried.

It defined him, but I was getting tired of letting it define me.

TWENTY-THREE
Inside Out

One pivotal night, something happened that would change life as I knew it. Some people in the class had organized a nurses' night out as we were ending one quarter of nursing school. It was a social night to get to know each other outside of school. Friends, family, and spouses were all welcome. I arrived at the venue, a karaoke bar, with my fresh-smelling, red-shirted, and hat-wearing hubby. It had been a while since we had been out on the town. This was sure to be a fun night.

We joined my classmates at a table lined with candles in the corner of a room. I was surprised a bar had real burning candles, creating a very cozy atmosphere. I had a designated driver, so I didn't hesitate to let the drinks start flowing. Heineken, appletinis, you name it; he was buying and I was drinking.

Then she walked in and happened to sit right next to me at the table to my right, while Ted sat to my left. I had silently wondered if she would show up. She always had a voice in the classroom, full of feministic views, which I much admired. I had engaged in a conversation with her once during lunch in the cafeteria at school, discussing the new female president of the college, with whom she said she was acquainted and then defended on several allegations. She had stressed how men couldn't stand to see a woman in a powerful position and would do whatever it took to bring her down. I had agreed with her sentiments.

There was something about the long red-haired woman that had made me unconsciously notice her, way before this evening. Now, here she sat next to me, very much in a party mood. The first thing she did was order a round of vodka shots for everyone at the table. More rounds followed, and I was completely consumed with her life story, which she had begun telling me in close proximity, as the place was loud.

As drunk as I was, I remember everything she said, from becoming a mother at a very young age, then getting a divorce not so long after, to what she had to do to provide for herself and her child, to the birth of another child much, much later. She explained how getting through nursing school was a lifelong dream, and how tough her life had been. We laughed and shared chicken wings, but the slight brush of skin as our hands met, trying to grab a wing at the same time from the same plate, had stirred an exciting awareness in me.

Why was I so taken by her, forgetting that the person who had escorted me here was sitting right to my left, completely ignored? We sang Fergie's "Big Girls Don't Cry" on stage, looking at each other as opposed to the crowd. We took trips to the restroom and danced arm in arm on the dance floor. The heat of her breath against my neck lit my body on fire. My every sense was heightened all of a sudden, smelling her perfume, noticing the shape of her body, the trace of goose bumps left behind on each piece of bare skin on my arms that her hands touched.

No man had made me feel this way.

I blamed it all on the alcohol. However, before when I drank too much, my senses were shattered. Tonight was the exact opposite. A heavyset girl of my race, also from my class, had at the start of the evening commented on how handsome my hubby was. I had joked, "You can have him."

She must have been keeping him occupied. Otherwise, I don't know how else he had let us continue with this seemingly innocent flirtation, until it got to the point he could no longer tolerate. She had been talking about her vacation to an island the very next day and had been insistent on taking a picture of my face with her cell phone, having me hold a candle to my face to provide some light for the flashless cell phone camera. At one point, she stepped out to smoke with the others. I would find out the next day from Ted how I had looked for her, like an infatuated teenager frantically looking for her boyfriend. On her return, she would come to me and hold my face so close to hers, kissing me on either side of my cheeks while apologizing for having left. Then, I guess, before our lips could touch, Ted had jumped from his seat and shoved her away from me.

Now clearly upset, he accused her of trying to seduce me right in front of him. She responded with just as much anger. He grabbed my hand and pulled me out of the bar. Nothing was said on the way home.

Wow, I sure am staying away from vodka shots, if that's what they make me do was what I was thinking, unaware of the seriousness of what had just occurred. When we arrived at our empty home, our kids were safely tucked away in beds at their gogo's house. I started to go through my phone, searching for her number, which I thought for sure I had saved. Ironically, I think by mistake I dialed Zoey's number at two in the morning and left a message that said how worried I was about her and how I hoped she got home safe.

When I vacated the bathroom and joined Ted in the living room, he was lying on the couch, with tears in his eyes. He surprised me with calmness on a night when I thought for sure his fists would meet my face. Maybe I was too incoherent for him to bother, or I had done a thing that had hurt him beyond belief.

The next day, I awakened, and my mind was rambling with the previous night's events. The small voice inside my head told me to deny, deny, deny, and blame it on the alcohol. Soon enough, he brought up the subject, recalling each and every move we had made. I did what the little voice had asked me to do and he was convinced.

I was concerned about the other party involved in the matter. I sent out a text, but I got no response back. When the two-week break was over and I saw her in class, she gave me a big smile and said, "Hi." I said hello back and the lesson continued. No one else brought up the issue. How was that possible? Had people not noticed the dramatic scene, or was I lucky and most of the people had left when it occurred?

I tried to clarify things with this person, but she avoided it at all costs. She went about like nothing had ever happened. She showed off her vacation fling in photos taken by the beach and told everyone how he would be coming for her graduation.

I let bygones be bygones, but my mind wouldn't let me sleep at night. A Pandora's box had been opened. The visions I had of this person and myself, I could not shake. Graduation was already approaching and the director of the nursing program had called me to her office once again. This time, she expressed to me Zoey's concern for her safety at the ceremony if Ted was present. This infuriated me. Am I not the student, and would this not be my graduation? If a teacher was worried about her safety, then she ought to stay home. Why was I being interrogated on this issue? This made me want to show just how perfect a couple we were.

At the pinning before graduation, Ted wore the finest suit to ever grace his body, and so did our son. Our daughter wore a pretty dress and there was a new outfit for me as well. As we walked in the corridor of the hall, where the nursing ceremony was being held, Zoey stood at a door, unable to escape our impending approach. I caught her looking; I caught Ted purposefully looking away from her direction, proving that their past had no bearing whatsoever on this present that he now possessed.

While standing in line next to the red-haired woman who had awakened the sleeping giant that resided in me, I could smell the vodka on her breath. I guess it was her birthday the night before. I extended a hug and a "Happy Birthday." I was a little unhappy with her choice of showing up not quite sober to this pinning ceremony.

As a practical joke, I had told my classmates that I would walk up to Zoey on stage and have her pin me, as we had been informed that we had a choice of walking up to any instructor we liked to give them the honor of placing the pin on us. I chickened out. My whole family was in attendance, and family friends were also here. Had I gone through with my planned act, it would have generated some giggling and laughter. I did not want to end things on such a note. I had nothing against the woman, nothing at all. Maybe in the future, whether we liked it or not, our children might forge a relationship. They're half brothers and sisters. I know if I had a way of knowing if any siblings were out there for me to connect with, I might make an effort. I've even gone on a quest to add anyone with the same last name as mine to my Facebook friend list in the hopes that we just may share a bloodline.

TWENTY-FOUR
Secrets Are Spilled

After I graduated from my RN program, things were progressively worse at home. I could not even bring myself to the occasional, once-every-three-weeks love session I had endured after every excuse had been used up.

One morning, after Ted had tried all attempts to be sweet and gentle to coax me into lovemaking—and those attempts had failed—he asked me what was wrong.

"You don't even make an attempt anymore. What's wrong with you? Do you want to be with a woman?"

I could not look him in the eyes, for I knew I had to admit it. I very softly explained to him how the incident at the bar had done something to me, how it had changed me in a way I couldn't explain—even though I had been aware of this side of me all along. In all my growing up, I had known women moved me in ways men never could. They did something to me that was beyond reason or explanation. I had known all along in my mind that I had a place of unexplained passion for the same sex that I had never dared explore or think about.

When I started to cry, he put his hands around me and consoled me. "I know what you're thinking."

WHAT? It's the same thing I say silently, and then I noticed tears in his eyes as well.

"Why are you crying?" I asked.

"Well, I know how you feel," he responded.

"You do? How?"

"Promise me that you will never use this against me. Promise you will never tell a soul what I am about to tell you."

At the time I made this promise to him, I had no idea he would try to take my life by beating me half to death.

I had no idea he would actually attempt to have me deported, take my children, and destroy every little thing I worked so hard for.

I had no idea just how cruel he could be.

I had no idea I would ever write my life story.

I really did not know that I would *need* to tell another soul about the things he was about to tell me.

I didn't know that I would eventually refuse to remain voiceless and silent about issues that matter.

And, beyond all that, my life matters.

Okay? I thought loudly inside my head, but I respond softly to his question.

"I think everyone goes through a phase of this curiosity at some point in their life."

"Have you gone through it?" I asked.

His sobs became intense as he hesitated, but he proceeded to explain himself. "I once almost killed myself over it."

"Over what?" I urged him to continue.

"When I was twenty-five, I don't remember where, but I had seen a movie with two men being sexual. After that, I became very curious about it. I was using a lot of drugs at the time and found myself at this porn store in Sioux City, where in a room a guy gave me a blow job. He even swallowed," he said.

This last part could have been left out, as he was sharing way too many details.

I didn't believe what I was hearing, but it did not stop there. He proceeded with some type of courage now, from my confession, I guess. He told me about how he had met a drug dealer when he first moved to Omaha. Back at his apartment, he had, in turn, given this man oral sex. He said all this with some excitement now, continuing to tell me the pet name for this guy's thing as well.

He also talked of the unwarranted attention he got from men when he was on the road. He confessed about how even throughout our marriage, he had to watch gay porn every three months to help him get off "really hard." It hit me: Ted is gay.

It explained it all, explained his past, explained his anger, explained his hate of the world and all who lived in it. This man was trapped. He had explained how knowing he wanted a family and wanted to be a good dad had helped him get over his attractions to men.

"I chose to have a family," he insisted.

Had he really? How many broken families had he created? Just out of instinct once, my friend Carol had said Ted was gay. Gay guys had not hid their attraction to him a few times when I was with him, out and about. It had never in a million years crossed my mind.

I think his sharing of this deep, dark, hidden secret with another soul was a release. He told me he feared that if I ever found out, I would leave him. His confession didn't make me want to leave him at all. He had actually opened up and freed himself for the first time in his life. He had made himself vulnerable, like any human being had to in order to be free.

It wouldn't be this revelation that made me want out. Rather, it was the wear and tear of years of insults and physical threat, the summons to pay his past debt from the early 1990s, the child support liens now placed on our mortgage. His hoarding of unnecessary junk, which had filled our basement, garage, and shed, made us look like pack rats.

It was the fact that I had been married to this man for over five years now and in all that time my children and my education were the only two positive things I had obtained. I had dealt with his baby-mama drama; I had dealt with his coworkers' drama. Yes, he couldn't keep even other guys around to work with. He had a huge fight with a guy named Tom while out on the road. Tom had called me and told me how Ted was impossible to work with, how rude he was even toward customers, and how embarrassed he often made him feel.

It was the fact that he had not made any effort at all in trying to fix his birth certificate, and that he had long ago screwed up his life so bad. Under the shadow of his past, he tried to make me think I could never become what I knew I had the potential to be.

I tried to pretend things were still normal. I tried to enjoy his efforts when he accompanied me to Lincoln to write my RN boards. We left the kids with my mother and he paid for an expensive room. We had a great dinner the night before my boards and he tried to touch me while we slept. All I wanted to do was avoid him like he was a bubonic-plague-infested rat.

My little attempts to please him left me feeling so nauseated that I heaved and had to excuse myself to the bathroom to puke. It couldn't be done. I couldn't make myself do it. I couldn't be with this man in a sexual manner if my life depended on it, not even for one last time. It was over; it was the end.

Aside from my own internal turmoil of my desire to be with another woman, my head was now clouded with images of Ted with a man—the place I now believed he really belonged, and not with me or any other female. I knew for sure that if we pretended to be these people we were really not, neither one of us would ever find happiness in this life.

Ted and I had been bound by our similar childhoods of neglect and dismissive, dismal parenting. Now we were bound yet again—but this time as outsiders who were denying their true sexual natures for some modicum of marital "unity."

That day in June, I told the inner Ruth that I would not be doing that again. With the stress of what was going on in my marriage, I sat down to take boards the next morning, with a heavy heart and an insomnia-induced headache. The other two students from my class, who had started at the same time as I had, were up and done in about forty-five minutes. I sat there for another four hours with questions that refused to cease. Sometimes the computer would go blank, making me hopeful about the end of this torture, only to indicate a break time, if I wanted to take the offer. When I declined, it would bounce back with IV calculations.

In my fourth hour, how could I think of any formulas? I got through it somehow. When I was out in my car, I fell over the steering wheel, convinced there was no way I passed that exam. It was, by far, the hardest academic test I had encountered. I had always been sure of my facts, my medical knowledge, and my understanding carved out of two years with some great nursing instructors at a great community college. Now it had come to this: failure.

The drive home was mostly quiet as I was consumed with dissecting every question I had answered, sure I had placed the wrong answer. At Aunt Norma's house, I hugged my children so tightly, in a way saying, *I hope you'll love me still, even after I fail my boards.* In another, I was saying, *I hope you'll love me still, for having the courage to end a marriage that should have never taken place.*

Norma gasped with my every expression as I tried to depict the toughness of the exam I had taken. She assured me that I made it, assured me not to worry. Like so many friends and family members, she believed in me way more than I believed in myself.

TWENTY-FIVE
Hollywood Gives Me a Sign

What was done, was done. I chose not to look up my results in the forty-eight hours they would be available online. Instead, I opted to go to Los Angeles for my cousin Octavia's bachelorette party. She had moved to Long Beach to join her longtime boyfriend, Ivan. They were soon to be wed. I was looking forward to this trip so much, thinking it might be just what I needed. If I could get away—just me, myself, and I—I could think clearly about one of the biggest decisions I was about to make.

With a hint of jealousy, Ted helped me prepare. We shopped for a classy suitcase and a few new clothes. I promised him that things might be better when I returned. I also encouraged him to take a trip to California to visit his best bud, Mike, for his birthday. It would be the first time I would be away from my kids for more than two days in a row. This made me miss them before I had even left.

I promised to take them on a vacation soon, maybe Disney. Chido got excited; Simba not so much. Simba had just turned two, and Chido was to be four in September. They both loved to talk, hardly allowing each other the time to chat without interruption. They were so close, but they had their share of fights, mostly over "my boy toy" and "my girl toy." As I departed Omaha, I made a conscious note in my mind to think of my children first, in whatever decision I ultimately would make.

A few delays, and being the passenger who was singled out for screenings at every airport, made the journey a long one. That was, until in a bookstore I had browsed the shelves and found a book entitled, *Same Sex In the City: (So Your Prince Charming Is Really a Cinderella)*, written by two girls, Lauren Levin and Lauren Blitzer, whose faces were on the cover. Embarrassed by the title of the book I was engrossed in, I folded the top cover so no peeping eyes could catch the title. Oh, how I related with the true stories in this book, or with the things I had misunderstood, or with the emotions I had been ashamed to admit, even just to myself. Other normal, healthy, and beautiful girls in the world had experienced what I thought only I had. Then came the coming-out stories or the finding out by accident of family members—the pain and agony it caused most Western-cultured, American, white families.

How would it be for me—a black, illegal African girl, with two kids and a psychotic spouse?

On my last leg of the flight as we descended onto the LAX runway and my phone had service once again, it signaled an incoming picture mail. I opened it, getting ready to stand and collect my carry-on luggage from the holder above. I could make out a certificate. *Why is Ted sending me a picture of our marriage license?*

I looked close, bringing the cell phone closer to my vision. I read the print *RUTH MARIMO, Registered Nurse License.* My obvious happiness made the lady next to me inquire about what was going on. She was the first person I told that I had indeed passed my RN boards. I was now a Registered Nurse.

I sent out a mass text; the deed was done; I had passed. Now I had a real reason to party while in L.A.

Octavia picked me up at the airport, looking lovely as always. She had visited us just the previous Memorial holiday in Nebraska. This was actually the shortest time we had gone without seeing one another. She had received the good news and they had a bottle of champagne waiting at their apartment to congratulate me. We stayed up late and caught up. I told her that there was potentially trouble in paradise, without disclosing the double jeopardy of homosexuality playing out between Ted and me. I did reveal all the other problems.

The next morning, we walked to the beach, five minutes away from where she lived. We snapped photos and had breakfast by the seaside. We toasted with mimosas and everything around was so renewing: the sound of the ocean, the conversation, knowing I now held an RN license. All these things made anything else disappear. I poured my heart out to her some more. She was so polite in her very British ways, apologizing after almost each sentence I told her. She would be celebrating her wedding soon, and I was filling her with the idea of ending mine.

So many things to see and places to go, we hurriedly returned to their place, which she occasionally referred to as a flat. We got ready to go to her friend Shira's house, where the party was being held. She looked absolutely stunning in her lavender party dress. I had black short shorts, which made me appear tall. This night was also exciting because after a good sixteen years, I was meeting my long-lost childhood friend Gertrude, who was now living in Valencia with her hubby and two kids.

The lights inside were switched off. There were little noises coming from inside the door; we paused; we were aware they were going to all yell out "surprise" when she entered the door. Sure enough, excited faces of a mixture of exotic-looking women warmly screamed their greetings. I sensed immediately the love these people had for their friend. Reena introduced herself first; then Shira, the host, did so, with a peck on the cheek. I liked her already. I was introduced as the cousin from Nebraska.

The food was exquisite, and the drinks were yummy. I loosened up; I was surprised by the compliments about my figure, especially after two kids. To me, these girls from L.A. looked as if they came out of magazines. Then Gertrude arrived and what a great feeling to see a friend again after so long. What an amazing feeling! We embraced, not believing it was happening. I introduced her to everyone, and the games and the show began.

Let's just say, what happens at Shira's house stays at Shira's house! Just know that it was a girls' night and they had fun like boys would have on a boys' night. The party continued at Club Ivar in Hollywood—with drinks and shots coming from each and every direction. I was later told that I had removed my shoes and danced all the way to the floor, backside in the air and all.

I don't remember getting back to Long Beach, but the next day I was safe and sound in Ivan and Octavia's apartment. She had forced me to drink water and lots of it before I had crashed. The following day, we drove to the Hollywood sign, where her cute Mazda overheated right at the bottom of the hill. I was quick to diagnose the problem after seeing the green liquid that was bubbling out of the hood of the car. We both had on short little dresses and flip-flops, not at all prepared for car trouble. I assured my cousin that all we needed was a little water and the car would still be drivable.

We made the hike to get as close as possible to this famous sign that I had long seen in movies as a kid back in Zimbabwe. Back then, I had no idea that one day I would be posing for pictures in front of it. When we made our descent, we drove to a gas station and refilled the coolant and headed out to Hollywood, where she took me to all the famous sites. We saw the Kodak Theater, the Hollywood Walk of Fame, the building that contained the ladder where Julia Roberts and Richard Gere had shot a scene for *Pretty Woman,* the Chateau Marmont Hotel.

We drove to Beverly Hills and Bel Air and saw celebrity homes, including the house from *Fresh Prince of Bel-Air,* which had always been one of my favorite TV shows. We parked and walked on famous streets, like Rodeo Drive lined with high-fashion and high-class stores, such as Gucci and Guess, and the hotel to which Richard had taken Julia. I had a chance to stop and shop for everyone back in Nebraska; my kids being first and foremost, of course.

Since my arrival in California, Ted had called numerous times, making it so obvious that he was having a hard time that I was gone and I was in a faraway place and actually having a good time without him. After his fifth or so call of the day, I had turned the ringer on my phone off and decided he would not spoil this lovely day I was having in this famous city. I still managed to pick out two T-shirts for him as well. After all, he had given me some of the money for my trip. That, after all, was what he was good at, giving me something so that at a later time he could then say, "Well, I gave you that" or "I did this for you." His giving anything was a means of control, which was why he eventually lost it when I stopped accepting anything at all from him.

We stopped at Neiman Marcus to pick up Ivan's suit, which needed adjusting. We had planned to go back to her flat and then get ready for the taping of BET's *Comic View*, which Octavia had tickets for. We had dinner with Ivan in Hollywood; but according to the dress code on the tickets for the event, no shorts were permitted, and that's what he was wearing. To solve the problem, he would have to wear his expensive suit with a T-shirt and no socks. He also kept his shorts on, putting pants on top. When we arrived at the theater, where the show was taking place, there was such a long line. We were clearly running late.

I was very astonished by how looks were everything in Hollywood. Earlier in the day, I had seen several blond women, with the same big fake boobs, tight faces, and plump lips. They all looked like they could be the same person. Octavia had referred to them as "Hollywood Bimbos." Now, at this show, looks would prove important again as a lady quickly approached us upon arrival with tickets she said are for the VIP. She wanted the three of us to be sitting in the front row for the taping of the show. This did not imply that we had incredible good looks, but rather that we were thin compared to the majority of people in line. Our appearance was a factor—a sad but true one.

My cousin had explained to me that looks and even race played a big difference in what one did in L.A. She said even clubs picked and chose who could come in based on looks. This crowd made it clear that there was also a racial divide in Hollywood, with nearly all the people in attendance for the BET show being black.

The comedians were very funny and the host, Joe Torry, was miniature in real life. He had somehow discovered that Ivan was not wearing socks and had joked and teased him throughout the show, even inviting him to the stage and making light humor of his British accent. We were prompted to laugh and to clap, which made me understand how unrealistic these shows were when they played on our television sets. The night out was a long and enjoyable evening, but finally getting to rest was a good idea.

As I settled down for the night, it occurred to me that the show had been a performance, even for the audience watching it. All of us in our lives are play-acting and pretending to be what we are not. My whole life had been playing a game of pretend: Pretend I am happy. Pretend I am here legally. Pretend I have parents. Pretend I am heterosexual. Pretend I was not in an abusive relationship. Pretend I belong.

We did as many things as possible on my short visit. *I will definitely return to this place* was my parting thought as I was shuttled to the airport on the day of my return home. I would run into delays once more, resulting in an overnight stay in Denver, which was hard and lonely, as I now missed my children so much. However, it gave me time to really think about my future. On the flight into Omaha, I firmly decided in my heart and mind that I had to find a way out of my marriage.

Instead of giving me a reason to stay in the marriage, my trip to Los Angeles had actually made me more determined to do just the opposite. The few days away from Ted's constant eye was a relief. Even when he was away on the road, he still inquired about my whereabouts. He called often throughout the day. When busy, if I forgot to say "I love you, too" at the end of the conversation, he would call back immediately, inquiring about why I hadn't said it. For the few days I had been away, I felt like I wasn't suffocating.

Yes, that was really the best term to describe what I had been feeling for many years with this man. I constantly felt like I was suffocating; I had a false sense of responsibility for his happiness. Since he was older, I thought he needed me to take care of him as he aged. I felt like if I left him, then he would be back where I met him—with nothing, in a dirty and dinky apartment.

What I realized while on my trip was that I was not responsible for anyone's happiness but my own and my children's, for that was what a parent did. I had to find inner happiness and peace in order for me to raise my children the best way I could.

PART three

Gaining Pride.

TWENTY-SIX
Gearing Up to Say Good-bye

There was no more pretense when I arrived back home in Omaha. On that very first day, I told Ted we were done. He endlessly asked why. He cried continuously. He was angry without bounds, but nothing about any of it was new at all to me. He had done this in the very first month of our relationship, and with every threat of my departure thereafter. I wasn't looking back, not this time. The more distant I became, the angrier he got.

I started hanging out with my friends again. Brenna and Lucy, with whom I worked at the nursing home, became the two people I was open with about what was happening in my life.

The day I sat my adoptive mother down and explained that I wanted out of my marriage, she cried so much. She cried a river for my children. She begged me to find a way for my children's sake. I confessed that was what I had done all along and it just wasn't working anymore.

I had gotten a raise now at work, with the passing of my RN boards. I was now working full-time and would slowly cut off any monetary assistance from Ted. I started paying the mortgage and bills, even though we lived under the same roof. One weekend I had spent the day at my friend Rachel's cabin by the lake, swimming and having fun, while Ted was home with the kids. He had made several attempts to call me, leaving a gazillion threatening messages.

When I returned home after dusk, the door was chained, but my skinny arms had the ability to unchain doors from the outside. I let myself in and he came to meet me at the door, fuming, "Why didn't you answer my phone calls?" I said nothing while he grabbed the phone from my hand and smashed it into the wall. Unsatisfied with the little damage he caused, he then stomped on it with his shoes, applying all his force, and the phone broke. He went on and on about how the phone was under his contract and how he paid the bill for it. He then said if I wouldn't pick up his phone calls, then I didn't need a phone. I slept in my daughter's room that night—something I had started doing whenever Ted was home.

Unable to stand the way I was outgoing now, he started to take the kids with him to Sioux City on the weekends. This was a relief because any night he was home was a sleepless night. He would often stand over my head as I slept and just scream at me about how I was making a mistake and how he would make me pay for it. The day after he smashed my phone, he had offered to get me a new one. I strongly refused, opting instead to refund him the money to cancel my phone under his contract. That very week, I signed up with AT&T and purchased a new iPhone; that independence made him mad.

I began to avoid being under the same roof with him, going to my mother's and staying there to avoid confrontation. I had always told Ted how important it was for our children to always have both of us in their lives, no matter what. With his past and his own childhood history, he understood the pain associated with growing up with an absent parent. When it came to the kids, I was with them while he was gone during the week; and on the weekends he would have them. No matter how bad I felt about my estranged husband, I never wanted to keep him away from our children. My theory was that it was better for them to know a bad father than not to know him at all.

I had come to the realization that I liked women instead of men. I was slowly starting to accept that fact within myself. I was on a quest to find out from other women if they had experienced these emotions and feelings I was discovering. I joined a few websites, setting up profiles, indicating I was curious and that I wanted to hear from other women like me. I never paid close attention to any of these profiles.

Whenever Ted was home alone, something would happen to the computer. A Trojan horse would somehow infect the computer after he used it. I knew by now that gay themes were of interest to him by his own admission, but it had to be more than just that. He had now become obsessed with trying to find out what I was up to. I had stopped talking to him after the cell phone incident. Equipped with my own phone in my name, he had nothing to hold over me.

Trying to come to terms with my own homosexuality was one thing, but now knowing that I had been married to a man who was most likely homosexual, or at least bisexual, presented a whole different emotional challenge for me. In my own defense, it had taken me all this time to come to terms with my sexuality. Ted had actually explored his homosexuality and had most likely been living on the down low (men who sleep with men secretly, while pretending to be straight). I was concerned about sexually transmitted diseases; even though as far as I knew, I hadn't contracted anything from him.

Ted would sift through the history on the computer. He would try to access my e-mail account, my Facebook, anything at all. One day, he discovered the profile I had created and threatened to tell the world I was gay and leaving him for a woman. I responded by saying that I would tell the world he was gay, too. He changed his mind and let it go. I knew that Ted would never want anyone to know about the possibility of him being gay or bisexual. I knew it was something he felt deeply ashamed about.

I received a message one day from one of the profiles. I had imagined that even if I had decided to say I am gay, how would I even find someone? I thought that a relationship would not ever be possible, and where would gay women come from in Omaha, Nebraska? But this girl sent me a kiss and I viewed her profile, and she looked nothing like a lesbian!

Of course, I still carried intense stereotypes and prejudices of my own regarding LGBTQ people. I held an ignorant belief that lesbians had to look a certain way, despite the fact that how I looked was not typical of how I thought a lesbian would appear. I added this woman to my messenger, and within days we began to chat.

I tried to be very honest with her from the start. I explained how long I had been married and that I was still married but separated. I told her all about my kids and my friends and the places in Omaha we hung out. Coincidentally, she hung out at those very same places.

Our conversations were very easy and honest and innocent. We both admitted how good it felt to talk to someone who was dealing with the same issues. She was a cute girl and told me about her prior relationships with men, and how she finally admitted to herself that she was a lesbian. For a while, we just happened to catch each other online and chat. She seemed such a genuine friend, with absolutely no agendas whatsoever. Our friendship was mutual and we discovered we had many things in common besides being attracted to the same sex.

In August, Ted visited his friend Mike in Pasadena. While there, he got a tattoo of our daughter, Lover Girl, on his chest. He sent a picture and I thought it was a nice gesture to show his love for his daughter. However, I also asked myself, *What about the rest of them?*

I hoped that going away would bring him some self-discovery, like my trip to L.A. had done for me. He returned and was the same angry guy I'd always known. By this time, I was completely removed from the relationship, which I did not miss. I did not miss him, since I was out of love. He still struggled with the fact that I wasn't going back to him.

Ted hated me so much that I feared that if I slept under the same roof with him, he might get a knife and stab me to death. Then he would bury me, where I would never be found, and make up a story about my hasty return to Africa. He had promised to do this to me many times in the past, but he always said those threatening scenarios were just jokes.

TWENTY-SEVEN
At Last, My First Time

On the occasions he seemed friendly since July, after my trip to L.A., Ted and I had hung out. We had gone to strip clubs and had gone dancing and talked about the future. He had asked me if I would want one day to settle down with a woman. I had been honest and said maybe. He vowed that would never happen, not over his dead body. I had tried to explain that my life was mine to live and not his to decide what I could do with it.

I had found this inner strength somehow to stand up to him. In his rage and anger, he would punch walls and doors. He would throw stuff, but I was not deterred.

I had agreed to finally meet with my new friend, who went by the name of "Chrissy." I would be in the downtown area with my friends Lucy, Xio, and Nicky, and I suggested we meet later on in the night. It was a girls' night out. I loved being able to go out and have fun with my friends. Lucy and Brenna had converted me to sushi months earlier and we would get together often for sushi night. On this night, however, we decided to eat at Old Chicago downtown. I spent the evening texting Chrissy back and forth, keeping her updated on my whereabouts. I was eager to meet a girl who was a lesbian and then become friends and help each other deal with this dilemma we shared.

Nothing about our conversations indicated anything more than the hope of friendship. We just were both excited to be two women in Omaha, Nebraska, who had reached the decision that maybe they were lesbians. Chrissy had told me in our chats that in a few months she would be moving to Arizona. She hoped she would be around more gay and open people, so she could live her life on her terms. Omaha just didn't have beautiful gay women, so she thought.

When my friends and I got to the club, it was packed. The Max is the biggest gay club in Omaha, with a very heavy presence of gay men. These guys dance like there is no tomorrow and walk around shirtless. What is it about gay men that gives them such confidence?

As we walked the dance floor, bodies were pushed together and we had to squeeze between them to get to the bar and order drinks. I had not yet revealed to Lucy, Xio, and Nicky that I was expecting to meet up with a friend here tonight. I was hoping to avoid their questions, as clearly this girl was just a friend. We danced and drank, and still my new friend had not shown up. Then my phone rang and it was Nicky. In the few minutes that she had disappeared from view, she had gone to the bathroom and had passed out, apparently from the heat in the place, because we knew she was not drunk. It was club policy to evict anyone who passed out, so there she sat outside, all by herself. I sat next to her and tried to find out what happened. I offered to take her home; but in the back of my mind, I was thinking that I wouldn't get to meet Chrissy then.

To my relief, someone was already on his way to get her. I felt bad for my friend. It had started off as such a fun night and now she had to go home, way before she intended. After she was picked up, it was close to midnight. I got a text that said, *I'm here now. Where are you?*

On the dance floor, on the hip hop side, getting a drink. What are you drinking? was my response.

Just water, come to the door.

I tried to make my way to the entrance as fast as I could. When I got there, I didn't see her. I knew from her picture that she was blond, with a cute face, but that was all I knew. I texted her to say I didn't see her and she responded to wait there, she was coming.

While I was busy looking down at my phone, this beautiful girl, with a radiant smile and lengthy, smooth legs, walked up to me and said, "Hi."

I froze, completely surprised by her appearance. I knew she was cute, but now that she stood before me in these shorts and heels, *WOW!* She was gorgeous, and I would be happy to be friends. Clearly, even if I was in a position to date someone, she was way out of my league. I shook off my obvious surprise and we started to talk, walking toward the bar. She explained she was with an ex and another friend, and that they were both after her.

At the bar, the guys she was talking about were all over her as soon as she appeared. One put his hand around her and another was acting like he was her man. I decided to walk off and find my friends, saying, "Well, maybe we'll catch up later." She was occupied at the moment.

Within a few minutes, she texted, *Where did you go?*

My reply was *I don't blame those guys for being all over you. You're so damn hot.* Or maybe not exactly in those words.

We met up in the bathroom and just started talking like we had known each other a long time. We went outside in the back and talked some more. She asked about my kids. I asked about her plans to move to Arizona. The conversation kept flowing. Then she asked if we could go somewhere quieter so we could talk some more. I said sure and suggested my house. My kids were in Sioux City with their father, I said.

We went back in and I tried to find my friends. I found them sitting at the edge of the dance floor. Since we had driven my car to get here, I stuttered a little as I explained that I would be taking this friend of mine home. They both gave me an inquisitive look, but they didn't say a word. I got my keys; but before we exited, we paused on the dance floor briefly and simultaneously we started to dance together. For the first time, our bodies touched, but we broke away and said, "Let's go."

Our conversation to my house is blurry in my mind, maybe because even though I knew this was purely innocent, I was slightly nervous knowing that I was bringing a woman who was also a lesbian into our home. Ted was spending countless nights on the road and most weekends out of town with the kids. I never questioned his whereabouts, never wanted to know if he was with someone, doing whatever.

I had separated myself from Ted at the beginning of the year. It was September 20, 2008. In my heart and mind, I had no emotional, physical, or spiritual ties to Ted. Legally, we were still married, but I had started the process of acquiring a lawyer. Because I knew that he would turn my immigration status against me, I had started to look into what options I had to obtain legal residency without him.

All of a sudden, my house appeared so messy, now that I had this beautiful stranger in it. In the living room, a big portrait of Ted and me in our early days still hung on the wall and family portraits were everywhere. I suggested a movie perhaps. She said sure and I put a DVD into the player. As I went to the couch to sit next to her, I picked her legs up to make room and placed them over mine. For the first time, our eyes met at close range. Nothing was said, but our faces kept coming nearer.

When our lips met, we both broke and pulled away, because something about kissing was making us both hyperventilate. I proceeded to undo her shirt and bra. Before my eyes, her perfect bosom stood at attention. Her rosy nipples invitingly stared back at me. At that moment, I felt my liver quiver. My body shivered with an instant fever.

Chrissy noticed I must be going into some type of cardiac arrest. She rescued me by whispering, "I know it's your first time. It's okay. I'll teach you how. It's okay."

As she softly instructed me of where and how to touch, I followed her orders, eliciting a loud and excitable moan—a moan that sounded like a well-orchestrated opera in my ears. This ability I now possessed to please her in this way sent waves to my spine. A river started to flow between my legs.

Am I urinating? No, a secret faucet had simply been turned on for the first time. Never in my life would I have ever guessed this would be possible. I'm not sure how we carried ourselves to the queen bed in my bedroom, where she took her turn at doing the things she had just taught me to do, completing this magical act with her soft face and the softest lips touching my other lips.

My excitement rose to a level that threatened to render me unconscious. I felt the biggest wave approach as I reached a climax. We both collapsed, exhausted, and completely out of breath.

That night, I made love for the very first time to a woman, whose beauty surpassed even my wildest imagination. Of course, I held her tight for the remainder of the hours to dawn, just in case I had dreamt it all.

TWENTY-EIGHT
Katy Perry Has Nothing on Me

Around noon the next day, we woke up and she wanted to hurry home. She had called her mother and said she was spending the night at a friend's. Since she was planning on leaving Omaha, she explained, her plan to pay off her debts first was the reason she was staying at home with her parents.

Nothing about what happened felt awkward. There was no inward guilt that either one of us would have felt, had the other person been a man. Intimacy with a man always made me feel bad about myself. The only way I can make any sense of that is the simple fact that I had tried to be a heterosexual person when I wasn't. The same way that many light-skinned members of my race had tried to pass for white, I had tried to pass for straight. I finally understood that when I was fully able to be myself and experience sexual and emotional intimacy with a woman, only then would all the dots connect. Only then, after I had been with another woman, did I finally understand all the uneasiness of being with men.

I simply was not created to ever experience that kind of connection with the opposite sex. The puzzle pieces of who I was as a sexual being were simply not designed to fit with those of the opposite gender.

I am not the only person who was created this way. There are countless people in the word genetically designed in exactly this same way. It is not a flawed design. It is just who we are. Unfortunately, we just live in a world that makes us reject ourselves and struggle so much to accept our innate truth.

Nothing about our being together was like anything I had ever experienced before. It made perfect sense. No part of my being, my essence, my body and mind, rejected any of it. I felt completely at peace. It felt like home to me—the home I had been searching for all this time.

I had discovered the thing that had been missing, the part of myself I had never found. Amazingly, it had been there all along.

When I dropped her off by her car, I was impressed by how chic her car was. We texted each other about how fantastic the experience had been for both of us. Even though she had been with other girls, she expressed that what we had was at a completely different level.

So now I had kissed a girl, and I liked it!

I knew after that, there would be no turning back. I tried to talk to several of my friends about this new person I was, or rather the person I had always been, without even knowing it. My best friend, Thoko, had doubted this theory of mine, insisting that since we were best friends in high school, and I had liked boys, I couldn't be gay.

"You just need to meet a nice guy, Ruth. You gave up on men because of your bad relationship with Ted" was her reasoning.

I also noticed off the bat that she didn't want her husband, Farai, knowing or finding out about the fact that I was telling her that I was gay. With a tone of hesitancy, she pledged her love and support for me, but it was difficult for my friends to acknowledge me. Even though they said they supported me, their responses were tinged with shame.

In the days that followed, Chrissy would come by my house and I would greet her at the door. Few words were ever spoken; clothes would fly off at amazing speed. I was much like a kid with a new toy—an insatiable new toy.

On our third meeting, after dinner at La Mesa, she accompanied me to pick up my kids from Norma's house. I had brought friends to her home plenty of times, so this wouldn't be new. I was waiting to see how Chrissy would react to seeing my kids, and how they would react to her.

Immediately she started a game of cat and mouse, chasing them about the place. They were running and giggling, trying to escape her grip. Then she would catch one of them and raise them up in the air; they would cry out with laughter for me to rescue them. Their mutual connection was so natural.

Had this been a man I was bringing into their lives, things would have been much different. I had never been one to trust men of any kind—even less so, strangers around my children. Seamlessly, I started this romance with this beautiful woman. While at work, I sent texts nonstop. After work, we talked on the phone. Almost daily, she would spend the evening with me and the children, helping with dinner and the kids' bedtime rituals. After the kids were tucked away, we would watch hours of *The L Word,* the most addictive show to anyone who has ever had any attraction to the same sex.

When the kids would spend weekends with Ted in Sioux City, they would return and talk about Latisha, with whom I assumed they must have been spending a lot of time. With Ted's sudden accusatory tone when questioning me about the possibility that I might be seeing someone, it was obvious that the kids had mentioned Chrissy to their dad.

The first time he asked me if I was seeing someone, I simply didn't answer the question. I neither admitted nor denied the allegation, pointing out to him the fact that he and I had been over for some time and that he needed to face that truth.

When I had confessed to Ted my feelings toward other women—on the morning he, in turn, made his confession to me—he had assured me that maybe we could find a girl we could both be with. That hypothetical solution would solve my dilemma; hence, his suggestion of visiting strip clubs together. However, he had been overly jealous at any slight attention the strippers had paid to me.

Ignoring the fact that the demise of our relationship had started a long time ago, he now used this new knowledge of my interest in women as an excuse and a means for where all the blame would lie. He had made a call to Norma, crying and telling her how I wanted to destroy our lives. My aunt had called me, pleading, saying she had never heard a man cry so much in her entire life. I told her that Ted was good at crying; it's what he had always done. He would choke the life out of me, then turn around and cry. I was numb to it all.

Chrissy, on the other hand, now had a change of heart. She hardened toward me.

Determined to leave Nebraska in the near future, she felt a relationship would not be in her best interest, so she began to act cold. On a day we met for a movie, I met her after work, still in my scrubs. I had bought flowers and a card. I guess I was trying to pull out all the stops. As we strolled in the mall, men watched her walk. Some literally snapped their necks, unable to remove their gaze from this Barbie-shaped, blond woman who walked by my side. I attempted to hold her hand in the movie theater and she pulled it back.

Later at home, I sent her a text inquiring about her rather aloof behavior. She did not want a relationship, just friendship. Okay, I wouldn't push it. But after an attempt to hang out just as friends, it was she who had been unable to stand the distance I had kept from her.

We went on a date, both dressed to kill in little black minidresses. We had dinner at Kobe Steak House, a cab ride downtown, barhopping, and walking the streets of downtown, arm in arm. Boys driving by were unable to control their whistles toward us. We were so flattered.

It was on this night she told me she was falling for me and might not be moving, after all. Being with Chrissy was the first time in my life I had experienced sexual intimacy in a completely uninhibited way. It was the first time nothing about having sex grossed me out or sickened me, compared to the countless times I had somehow felt violated whenever I was intimate with the handful of men I had gone this far with in my life. Even when I had enjoyed it, it never felt right, ever.

With Chrissy, during most nights together, we just would never sleep. Addicted to each other's bodies, we would make love to the point of utter exhaustion and injury, bruising pubic bones and almost dislocating hips. Even while driving sometimes, she would take my hand, unzip her pants, and please herself with my fingers, while my other hand controlled the steering wheel. She was too impatient to wait till we actually got home.

It was euphoric, the kind of lovemaking I had only read about in books. Sex had never been so powerful or meaningful in my life before this. It was so powerful that even later on in our relationship when we would argue, I could usually end the argument by touching her in ways I knew she couldn't resist. Sometimes she would cry in anger, but she would never ask me to stop.

We were making love the first time Chrissy told me she loved me. Tears streamed down her face. I teased her about that moment for months to come, imitating her moans of pleasure as she uttered the words. I teased her good-naturedly, of course. No one had ever loved me that way or at least expressed love to me in that way. It was deeply profound, and my teasing was an awkward and knee-jerk reaction to this overwhelming, new experience. It had been the most moving, erotic moment of my life—one I will never forget.

I even wrote her a letter, desperately trying to put my emotions and her impact on me into some kind of understandable language. Chrissy had opened my legs, my arms, my eyes, my mind, and my heart to possibilities I never envisioned.

That's how complicated my world was now. I was daring to indulge in the part of me that always existed, but I was also endangering my life. I was still married to a man whose anger was unsurpassed.

He would, without a doubt, make my life a living hell.

TWENTY-NINE
His Fists Rain Down on Me

I was now working on the cardiac unit at a local hospital, doing three-day, twelve-hour shifts a week, while picking up occasional eight-hour shifts at the nursing home in order to afford the mortgage and $300-a-week child care at La Petite Academy for my two children. It had been about five months since Ted had offered any help with any of the bills. Since I thought I could do it on my own, he was going to show me that I couldn't.

On the days I worked at the hospital, still in orientation, I would get up at four forty-five in the morning, shower, get my kids' teeth brushed, faces washed, and dressed. Then armed with their warm strawberry milks, we would head out south to their day care. I would then take the opposite direction, north, to my new job, which was a distance from where we lived and where day care was.

November 9, 2008, was the day of his most brutal attack on me. I cannot say I had known this day would come, in the way it came. I knew there would be an eventual showdown—I just never envisioned this.

It was a Sunday and Ted had not shown up all weekend, not even to get the kids. It was after ten at night and the kids were fast asleep, both of them in bed with me, for we would have an early day the next morning.

In my sleep, I could hear the door opening downstairs. I had locked and chained the front door, so Ted was letting himself in through the garage door.

The next thing, he was standing above me, mad, and screaming at me. "You have another thing coming! You know that? Reality is going to hit you real hard. This is the biggest mistake you ever made, and I will make you regret the day you were born."

"Okay, Ted, do whatever you need to do. The kids and I are sleeping, and we have an early day tomorrow. Please just let us sleep."

"Get out of that bed right now. Those kids are mine, not yours. Their name is Browner, not Marimo. They're Americans, okay? Not Africans! You hear me." His tone was getting angrier, his voice rising.

"Please, Ted. You can't wake the kids. Please, can you just let me sleep? I have to work in the morning."

"Well, I have all your documents, and you're going to pay, Africa."

I could see that he would not leave it alone. I decided to get up out of bed to remove the noise from the room and avoid disturbing our slumbering angels, because that's exactly what they looked like in their sleep. The children were so peaceful and so free, with no idea what was about to take place in their home, between the two people who had brought them into this world.

As I was walking, he was shadowing me. I was inquiring about the whereabouts of my documents. As I reached the kitchen, I turned to face him. Without hesitation, he kicked me in the torso with a boot-encased foot. I landed hard on the ground.

He followed me there with a barrage of fists. I did my best to cover my face, but it seemed to be his main target. He punched me with such force and power. He stood and replaced his fists with his boots, pounding at my head and face, then my torso. I started to beg him, please not to kill me.

I had never seen him this enraged. His entire face and neck looked red. He was shouting obscenities and telling me that today was my dying day. I believed him. He was much too strong for me to try to fight. I was simply holding on to life, glad that at least my children were sleeping and not witnessing this.

Seemingly tired of punching and kicking me, he grabbed my throat with both hands and he started to squeeze. I was twenty-eight years old and this was the way I would die. I felt my life slipping away. I became dizzy and faint. I could no longer resist or try to shield myself. I was lying limp on the ground, reduced to a dwarf by this man who had transformed into a Hulk-like figure right before my eyes. I was not sure how much time went by, but he released me, as if transformed back into a human being.

He frantically searched for the phone to make a 911 call. I lay motionless for a few minutes, but I could hear him telling whoever was on the other line about how I had attacked him with a knife and how he tried to defend himself. Something moved me to get up off the ground. My head was heavy and pounding, as if I had been struck with a hammer. There was chocolate pudding smeared all over the tiled kitchen floor.

I found my phone to make a 911 call to say I had been beaten. I ran outside the front door in an effort to find safety. I could feel my forehead swelling. Flashing lights appeared in both directions of Parkview Boulevard.

An officer ran toward me with something drawn, asking, "Where is the knife? Drop the knife."

"I have no knife. He is lying. I never had a knife."

"Let me see your hands."

I put both hands up, as if in surrender, to show the approaching officers that I was not the threat my attacker had painted me to be. As the first officer got close to me, the first thing he said was "Wow, your head is swelling!"

"Can I get some ice?" I asked.

"Stay out here. We will get it for you."

The cop entered the premises, while another started to question me about the events that led up to this point. I told them my version, which was, of course, entirely different from the one Ted was telling the officers inside.

The officers traded places. The ones inside came out to question me, while the ones questioning me went inside to question him. Someone gave me an ice pack, which I held to my bulging forehead. My head felt bumpy everywhere I touched. My right eye began to shrink. The officers spent about forty-five minutes investigating both our stories and the scene. They came out and told me that they had decided to put him under arrest. He had yelled something about me being an illegal immigrant the minute the police had arrived. I was escorted to my basement in order to be out of his path as they escorted him to the waiting police car.

After one officer took him away, a female officer and another male remained behind. They took photographs of my bruised face and body and the chaotic mess in my kitchen. I wrote a statement of what had occurred. After the police left, I got a call from a volunteer with a group that has to do with domestic abuse, inquiring about directions to my house.

At first, I thought I just wanted to go back to bed and forget that this night ever occurred. But then I realized that more than ever I needed to hear what these women had to say. So, at well after one in the morning, these two women, whom no one would be paying, were leaving the comfort of their beds and homes to come and sit down with me and give me some comfort. They introduced themselves and explained what they did. They had handouts explaining the cycle of abuse, which I was much too familiar with. In nursing school, I had gone over it all as well.

That was the jarring thing about domestic abuse. It did not discriminate. It mattered not who you were, or how educated you were. For most women all over the world find themselves in that very predicament, with no way of getting out. So as hard as this was for me, and for as long as it had taken, because of the near-death experience that had taken place, maybe this cycle would be coming to an end for me.

They advised me about protection orders and Victims' Witness providers and the rights I had as a victim. When they left, I thanked them and made the necessary call to Aunt Norma. I thought about phoning Chrissy, but why would I want to do that? She would be frightened soon enough. I also called work to let them know I would not be in the following day.

The next morning, Ted's work van was gone. I knew he had been bailed out. First thing on my list was getting a protection order. I sat down with the lady at Victims' Witness explaining what had occurred, even though the evidence was on my face. I had briefly looked in the mirror and had seen the horrors of his punishment. My right eye was bloodshot. I had a hornlike bump on the left side of my forehead. My arms had bruises and welts, as did my chest and side of my belly, my thighs and legs. My body looked like that of a whipped slave who had tried to escape and got captured.

There was no way I could hide this from my small children. The moment they noticed the change in my face, my kids had both asked what had happened. I was honest. I told them their dad had attacked me.

"My daddy mean to you, Mommy. My dad bad boy" was my son's response. These were words he would utter often for months and months to come.

Having turned four, two months prior, Chido was more mature in her response. Apologizing for her dad's behavior, and just wanting me to feel better, she reassured me by saying, "You'll be okay, Mom. I'll take care of you, okay?"

This made me feel so guilty. As parents, we're never to burden our children, especially four-year-olds, with the idea that they somehow are responsible for our well-being.

When filling out the protection order forms, I made it a point that I wanted him away from the children as well, unsure of his next move. The judge had reviewed and granted the protection order on the very same day I made the application, keeping him away from the kids and their school and Norma's house for ninety days and from me as well. I would have to go before the judge in person in about two weeks to prove the validity of my request.

Chrissy was shocked about what had happened to me. She spent the day with me at my aunt's. On the third day after the attack, I grappled with constant headaches and vertigo. I decided to go to the ER. The CAT scan showed extensive internal bruising of the face and head, but no broken bones. My bruises had become more evident now, despite my dark skin tone. So, as advised, I had gone to the police station to be photographed again.

In the weeks that followed, like I had suspected he would do, Ted had made an attempt to pick up the kids from school, even though they had changed his door code on the day I had given them the protection order barring him from picking up the children. Another parent had unknowingly allowed him entrance and the director of La Petite had stopped him with Chido in tow on his way to get Simba from his class. When she informed him that he would not be permitted to leave with the children, he had become frustrated, prompting them to give me a call at work. I phoned the La Vista police department as a result. At the realization that police would be involved, Ted left without putting up much of a fight.

He also would text my thirteen-year-old cousin, Tashinga, telling her of the things he had bought the kids, which was rather bizarre. It felt so liberating not to have him contact me in any way, but it also felt painful that he was not having any contact with the children.

When I had initially approached Ted about separating, I had made it clear that it was important for our children always to have us both in their lives, despite how we felt about each other. I had also offered him the house, noting that he was much older than I, and had many children and needed the home more than I did.

Norma and I had gone out of our way to set up meetings with Realtors to help us with this transition of getting my name somehow off the house and having Ted's name on it. After all, it was his child support liens that were on the mortgage.

At the meeting, Ted had been so rude, wanting to make a point of how much he had supported me through school and how now I wanted to leave him after using him. I always wondered at these times how he could have forgotten that I married him when he was jobless and that he had moved in with me with just the clothes on his back. It had been my support and encouragement that even made it possible for him to start making money and for him to have a house and junk cars to work on.

I kept my mouth shut in the meeting, embarrassed by the show he was giving. Never in my entire life had I seen a grown man act like such a toddler; a grown man who never, ever found fault in himself; a grown man whom everyone else wronged; a grown man who always had the short end of the stick.

After his departure from the meeting, the lady had tried to make light of his behavior by saying divorce was hard. I had never intended before the attack to keep my kids away from Ted. From my own experiences, I thought it was better for children to know the monster that their parents were than not to know them at all. I was caught between my need for safety and wanting not to keep them away from him.

When I returned to court for the extension of the protection order, Ted did not show up. The judge stressed that Ted could contact me in regard to the children, but he never attempted. I was granted protection from him for the next year and temporary custody of our two children for the next ninety days. However, it would be foolish of me to think even for a single second that Ted would allow this to happen.

Even after gaining the protection order, I always felt fearful, afraid that Ted would do something either directly or indirectly to me. I knew without a doubt that he would try to make me disappear. My mind would tirelessly go back to every threat he had promised since the beginning of our relationship.

THIRTY
A Chilling Knock

Knowing my immigration status was out of order, I was now in panic mode, trying to figure out a way to protect myself. Norma went to the immigration headquarters and inquired about ways she could help me, since she had permanent residency. They said it would not be possible for many reasons and that only Ted would be capable of helping out. They gave her a list of organizations and immigration lawyers who could take on the task of assisting me.

After giving me the list, I called every place and told them my story. Finally Catholic Services responded by saying they could maybe assist me. I set up a meeting with Josie, who told me about my two options. The first one, and most suitable to my case, was the VAWA (Violence Against Women Act). It would allow me to adjust my illegal status and, once granted, would permit me to have a green card without working with my estranged husband in any way. I just needed to have proof of marriage, proof of his citizenship, and proof of abuse. There was also the UVISA, which had to do with aiding in the prosecution of a criminal. Since it was not ideal for my case, we did not discuss it in detail.

She said I qualified for their services, given my background. I had brought documents along: my kids' birth certificates, our marriage license, and my protection order. She assured me she would immediately start working on my case. She would contact the police department, the hospital, my workplaces, as well as a lady from the Nebraska State Board who had called me, informing me she had copies of my documents, which had been sent to her by Ted. She had also informed me about the formal investigation that was being opened in regard to my immigration status and my nursing license.

Somewhat convinced that I was out of the water, I relaxed and was hopeful that finally I would have a chance to adjust my status and live in this country legally. That expectation would not be the case.

On December 31, 2008, I was awakened by a ruckus outside my bedroom window. The noise of people talking had also awakened Chrissy, who lay next to me. I got out of bed and walked to my bedroom window and looked out. Two black cars were parked behind my Red Nissan and Chrissy's white Honda. On the street, an SUV was also parked. I couldn't tell how many Immigration and Customs Enforcement (ICE) agents were out there, milling about, wearing badges and bulletproof vests.

My heart immediately sank. I knew exactly who these people were and, furthermore, who it was that they were after. The knock came. Chrissy, bewildered and worried, demanded to know what was happening.

"I don't know. Stay here" was all I could say. When I answered the door, an imposing redheaded man had a large image of me on his clipboard.

"Are you Ruth Marimo? Can we talk to you about the protection order you have against your husband?"

This was an unnecessary lie for him to tell. It was Ted who had brought them to my door, so I knew they were not at all concerned about the protection order I had against him.

When three of them let themselves in, two men and a woman, one man remained outside. In case I tried to run for it, I guess. Before they even began to interrogate me, I begged for them to let me tell my sleeping friend to leave. The red-haired man, instead, demanded she join us all in the kitchen.

"No, I insist this has nothing to do with her. I want her to go," I stressed.

The lady interrupted her colleague. "Okay, tell her to go."

I went back to the bedroom and said, "I'll explain everything later. Please do me a favor and leave."

Chrissy tried to protest; but from the look on my face, she seemed defeated and threw on some clothes. She made her way out, passing through the demeaning figures who stood in my hallway. I managed a quick hug. I could see the guy outside go after her toward her car.

I took a seat at the kitchen table. My heart was pounding; my rib cage was almost giving way.

"What's your legal status here, ma'am?" was the first question.

I answered honestly, telling them all about where my status was and my recent attempts to adjust it through Catholic Services.

They next inquired about my job. Again, I was stupid enough to be honest.

When a person is arrested, the police usually say, "Whatever you say can and will be used against you." I found out the hard way that this was true. I thought by being honest, I was helping my case, but I only made it worse. I should have kept my mouth shut and let them figure out everything—as that was their job, not mine.

The tone and stature of the red-haired man was so cold and chilling. His look reduced me almost to tears. The other guy asked about my kids, commenting how my son looked just like Will Smith's little boy in the movie *The Pursuit of Happyness*. How ironic that I found myself in this real-life situation—all for the pursuit of happiness.

After a grueling session of questions, I was informed that I was under arrest. I would be going with them to the immigration headquarters. I offered Norma as the person to stay with my children. I was allowed to make a call to her. I simply asked her to come over. It was early in the morning and she wanted to know what was wrong.

"Immigration is here" was my response. When I tried to communicate better in my native language, Shona, the red-haired agent became annoyed and threatened me to only speak in English.

Luckily, Norma arrived equipped with her identification and Social Security card, which was immediately demanded of her upon her entry. My adoptive mother tried to plead my case, to no avail. When she inquired about what was to happen to me, she was told, "She is being placed in Removal Proceedings."

My mom began to sob and I tried to comfort her. Still unmoved by what was happening, I asked if I could kiss my kids good-bye. Surprisingly, my kids and nephew had been good and remained in Chido's room, playing. My son wrapped his tiny arms around my neck, refusing to let go when I told him I had to go. I could see the female agent tearing up like I was; a teardrop ran down her cheek.

It was the most comforting thing that had happened to me that morning: to know that she could in a way feel the pain I was feeling. She recognized how helpless I was, and was able to be moved by a mother saying good-bye to her children. I don't know her name, but her vulnerability for my cause touched me. It made me see that she was just doing her job, that our humanity was not separate. She made me feel human.

What woman in this world would not be emotional while watching a mother separated from her children in this way? If I had been apprehended in the middle of committing a crime, then I would have deserved it. I was being taken from the comfort of my home. If there had not been a relative available to take my children, they would have been taken to some social service agency somewhere and placed in foster homes. Like so many American children who went through that system, their futures would have crumbled just like that.

Chido wanted to know if I would pick them up from Gogo's. I didn't know if I would. I didn't know if and when I would see these smiling faces of the people I loved the most in this world. As the lady followed me to the bedroom, where I would get changed, tears were now running down my face. She was empathetic, kind without expressing the words.

The red-haired agent was at least kind enough to handcuff me once I was in the SUV, away from my little kids' confused stares. Aunt Norma—the only mom I had known—yelled words of comfort, telling me not to worry about the children and how she would get me out, hopefully even by the end of the day.

I guess I had known from the very day I had gathered the courage to tell Ted that I couldn't do it anymore that this day would come. I just had not imagined it coming so soon. At the Homeland Security Headquarters on H Avenue, my belongings, my iPhone, and a piece of paper were placed in a plastic bag. My driver's license was taken and I was asked to remove my warm coat and was placed in a room with concrete benches and a toilet, with only partial walls giving it any sort of privacy.

The temperature in the room must have been set at thirty degrees; it was so cold. I wished they had allowed me to keep my coat. Instead, I grabbed one of the two worn-looking, old blankets in the room. The television set up above was tuned to a Spanish channel, indicating the majority of people this room housed on a regular basis. I would sit for what seemed like hours, unable to put my mind to rest. I thought about my children. I thought about my nephew and my little sister Tashinga. I thought about Chrissy and what she had witnessed early this morning.

I was later called out of the room toward the end of the day, for most of the workers had left the building. I had been offered a khaki bag with a sandwich, but I had refused it, unable to stomach anything. The two men who had apprehended me took me to a room, where everything was being recorded, and further interrogated me. Again, I talked, instead of remaining mute.

When it was all said and done, I was informed that my bail was set at $25,000. Unlike in the regular courts, where 10 percent could be sufficient for bail purposes, here it was the full $25,000 that was required.

Before this, I was working as an RN, saving American lives. I had paid taxes since my very first job in this country. I had worked long and hard and put all my heart into every job I ever had. Besides my immigration status and my inability to disclose the truth about that—in order to survive—I had always been honest with everything else I did.

I was a model worker—ironically, a model citizen. I had even saved a choking baby! I had made people's lives better with my care as a nursing assistant, then as a nurse. Still, here I sat, not having killed anybody or stolen from anyone, having been legally married and still married to an American citizen for almost six whole years. My husband had the power to put me in a cold room with nothing, and it would require $25,000 for me to even get out of that situation.

Did life have to be that unfair?

I was allowed a call to Norma to tell her of the bail amount. My conversation was cut short as my time was up. An African-American agent of light complexion drove me to my new destination, Cass County Jail in Plattsmouth, Nebraska. I had been asked to sign a form either saying I wanted just to be returned to my country of origin or that I wanted to be placed before a judge within ten days if I thought my bond was set too high. The second option was the box I had ticked and signed.

The thought of my immigration status ever being discovered and my being arrested had always been my greatest fear. It had been a part of me ever since I went out of status after my visitor's visa expired. The fear grew tenfold when I made the decision that I could no longer stay in the marriage I was in. I deeply feared my spouse would use it against me, and I was correct to fear that much.

All people who live illegally in any country carry this fear with them every day. We try to blend in with everyone else, but the fear of being found out is always eating away at us deep down. It is something I am thankful that my children will never have to experience, at least here in the United States. It is not something I wish on anyone. It is something I wish I didn't have to live through.

During the forty-five-minute drive to Cass County, I passed by the highways I had traveled on many occasions, including one that led right to Norma's Papillion home. I wished the driver would just turn and drop me there so I could be reunited with my children.

This was a dream that would not come true.

THIRTY-ONE
My Birthplace Is My Crime

Upon arrival, I am placed in a cell adjacent to the front desk, where a skinny, tall, and pale lady worked, trying to get me booked. When she instructed me to come out, she said, "So your crime is not being born here, I see."

I nodded and she tried to engage in light conversation, as if wanting to make me feel at home, despite my circumstances. She took my mug shot and my fingerprints again. They had taken countless numbers of my fingerprints at the Homeland Security Headquarters, but I guess it was not enough.

From looking at my hundred-pound frame, she guessed I was a size small. Even though she handed me the smallest size they had available, it still looked too big on me. I was given my orange T-shirt, shirt, and bottoms, which were labeled in large, bold black letters, CASS COUNTY JAIL. My belongings were placed in a labeled plastic container, and I was also handed a green container. Inside it was a miniature toothbrush and toothpaste container, a thin bar of soap, a towel, a plastic cup, and nothing else. On top of the container were a thin mattress, a thin brown sheet and bottom sheet, and a thin blanket. "Okay, Ruth, take your things and follow me to the mod," the lady commanded.

The mod was the sleeping quarters that held all the female inmates at this jail. It had steel bunk beds lined in rows, with nothing separating them. It was a large open area, not providing privacy or personal space. I tried to pick up my new possessions, but I failed. The weight was too much for me. She offered to help me carry half the things. Doors were unsecured as we approached them.

After taking the flight of stairs, I stood next to the steel bunk, which was to be my new bed. I was glad to be skinny, not knowing how else a body bigger than mine in size was expected to fit these tiny bunks.

OUTsider

The lady guard left and I found myself surrounded by strangers, also wearing orange jumpsuits like mine. I made my best attempt to make the bed—I mean, my mattress.

There was a very young-looking black girl, three white girls, and a much older Hispanic lady. One of the white girls came over and introduced herself; she seemed sweet. We started to talk. I told her about my situation; she told me about hers. Drinking and driving was the reason she found herself behind the walls, like two others in the mod. I was surprised that the reason one of them was there was her inability to come up with $500 to post bond. She had spent five long months behind bars for lack of having $500.

Behind these walls, it mattered not who I had been. Now I was just the same as any other criminal here.

I had been allowed one phone call on arrival, which I had made to Norma, giving her the name of the institution that now housed me. She was at the immigration lawyer's office. Mr. Pheiffer had briefly come on the phone and told me of his plans to get me out as soon as the following week. Since today was Wednesday, with only two days before the weekend, he doubted he could do much. With the knowledge that I was only in here till the weekend was over, I remained calm. I was very optimistic that I would soon be outside these walls and fighting to remain here in this country.

I quickly learned that this was actually home to some of the other girls, and they had claimed it to be so. They made all the decisions regarding what the rest of the mod was watching on TV, or what games were being played. I just wanted to learn more about the routines in this place, like visitation and so forth. Visitation for the women was every Monday and Friday for an hour, and visitors were to be there at least fifteen minutes ahead of scheduled visitation time to be allowed access. The phone in the mod allowed you a two-minute call to each new number, after which the person called could set up an account to receive more calls from you.

With no calling card to call Norma or anyone else, for that matter, I simply prayed that she would call and inquire about visiting times and I would see her face that coming Monday morning.

The food was bland and the coffee cold in the mornings. I lost my appetite with the first meal I had in this place. That first night, it wasn't anxiety that kept me awake but the sheer cold. What was it with the cold temperature in these places? As if being there was not enough, they had to insure the temperature was always freezing cold. I tried double-folding the thin blanket and making sure my head was completely submerged underneath it, to no avail. The nightly cold was relentless; and even during the day, I would find myself shivering.

I worried not, for Monday would soon come and my adoptive mother would have some good news about my release. I would then have my gorgeous kids in my arms again. Monday morning came and the girls readied by requesting razors with the morning rounds, together with fresh towels and underwear. The brown underwear could be changed each morning with the towels, but everything else—bottoms, tops, and sheets—was changed once a week, blankets once a month. By the time I took my shower, the water was cold. The spout of water would spray for two-minute intervals at a time, then shut off. One needed well-coordinated maneuvering in order to actually take a shower.

The guard came in and called out names for the first visit. Mine was not on the list. On the second visit, again my name was not called out. For the first time since getting there, I cried, hiding in the bathroom stall. I cried, missing my children, missing Norma, missing my friends, missing Chrissy, with whom I had no contact at all since her forced, rushed departure on the morning of December 31. I couldn't believe how much I needed my aunt—my mother—at that very moment, how seeing her face would have made all the difference in the world for me.

After noticing my long stay in the bathroom, the older Mexican lady, who spoke very little English, came in and tried to console me with signs. She pointed to the sky, to God, and pleaded with me to stop my crying, even though she now was crying, too.

When I gained my composure, one of the girls returning from her visit informed me that her parents had seen my crying mother walking toward her car after being informed that she was too late. Norma wanted me to know she had put some money on my books and had attempted to visit, but she was unaware of the fifteen-minute rule. I felt a bittersweet relief knowing that she had made an effort, knowing I had family here, someone who cared.

For commissary, we ordered on Mondays, which would be today, but orders would only be delivered on Thursdays, four long days from today. I ordered two calling cards, a packet of candy, envelopes, and a writing pad. During my stay in jail, writing became my sanctuary, my means of escape, the only thing that maintained my sanity.

That very Monday, I got over my disappointment of a missed visit by getting to participate in something that had been a childhood passion. I got to play basketball during the recreational hour. I also managed to get a few books from the small collection of books in their tiny library. So each day, like clockwork, the thing I looked forward to the most was playing basketball.

I thought of my Honey Girl and my Handsome Boy often, wondering what they would be doing at that very moment. I would also force myself not to think of my children, for thoughts of them brought such deep sadness and left me unable to control my crying. To hide this sadness, I would cry silent tears each night underneath my covers; then I would finally fall asleep, weeping.

I often dreamt of Chido and Simba running to me, their arms wide open, their smiles flashing white square little teeth and their laughter filling the air. This was a recurring dream, a dream that gave me hope, but it left me upset upon waking up and realizing that I was still stuck in jail.

On borrowed paper, the day after my incarceration, I had written a letter to my new best friend and the very first woman in my life, Chrissy. I apologized frantically for the scene that had taken place in her presence, somehow trying to explain my situation and my innocence. I pledged my love, but I also admitted that it was possibly over, voicing my understanding if her decision was not to continue this anymore. I was sure that was what she would be forced to do.

It was hard enough that her parents were Mormon and disapproved of homosexuality, period. Her mother had discovered her daughter's sexuality when she was alerted by the marks on Chrissy's neck. After realizing Chrissy had said she was with me, her mother put two and two together. The results had been akin to a funeral. Her mother had cried with such disappointment. It was bad enough that Chrissy's brother and only sibling was gay, but now her beautiful, blond daughter was suffering the same fate.

Then there was the fact that I was black, and I had two kids, and I was not divorced yet. Chrissy's paternal grandparents were from Germany. Her grandmother, whom I had met already, still had a very heavy German accent. I would have been lying to myself if I thought for one second my race was A-OK with her family. Even if I had been a black man, I knew it still would have been an issue.

Now, just how many knives can one mother be stabbed with? Above all that negativity, here I was an illegal alien, a criminal of some sort. As much as Chrissy might have thought she loved me, I could not fathom how her family would offer any support with what I was going through.

To my surprise, when I had called her phone again, checking if she had placed money for me to make the call, she was angry that I even thought that things would be over between us. She went on to say how she was prepared to sell all her belongings and move wherever it was that they would send me. Her family in the background had also offered words of strength and encouragement. It felt so unbelievably good to have anyone at all see me as innocent, to have her and her family's support.

By the third day, Norma had also placed money on her home phone. Talking to my kids was heavenly. Chido still wondered when I would pick them up and was still completely unaware of her mother's predicament. I told them both how much I loved them infinitely, and how much I just wanted the best for them. Knowing my children were in my mother's care, where I could at least speak to them from time to time, made me sleep a little better at night, but it would not last long.

The first Friday Norma made it on time, I told myself to be as strong as possible during our meeting so she would not worry so much. It had only been a week, but I knew I had already started to lose weight, as if it were possible for someone my size to lose any more pounds. I had stopped waking up for breakfast, but someone would leave their milk at the end of my bunk. Sometimes there would be more than one carton of milk. Milk became my staple food. The rest of the meals I would offer up to anyone who wanted a second helping, and someone always took me up on the offer. There was no way of getting any information about my case from the guards, as they did not have anything to do with people on immigration hold.

"We're just housing you" was what I was told often. Hearing my name being called out for a visit was like hearing my name being called out as the winner of an Academy Award. I was ecstatic to be able to see Aunt Norma again, even through a glass and speaking to her through a phone. My aunt-mother assured me that the kids were just fine and going to school like normal. She had paid the weekly tuition for them to continue going. She informed me that my lawyer had filled out the necessary paperwork to represent me and a petition for a bond reduction. I was amazed at how put-together she was, praying with me to be strong more than ever and just to believe that I would be getting out soon.

I would later find out that after these visits, which she made every Monday and Friday of each week for the thirty days of my immigration hold, she just broke down, crying on the phone for hours to anyone and everyone who listened.

My old roommate, Grace, also managed to visit me. Thankfully, I had put her on the list. As more and more Zimbabweans heard the news about my plight, people started gathering at Norma's house, bringing food and holding prayer sessions for hours on end. When I called, I got to talk to many of them, each one giving words of wisdom and strength.

I had never before in my life seen people come together in this way, and all for me. The support was overwhelming. Some donated money, hoping my bond would get reduced and I could soon join them. My mother had initially tried to keep it a secret that I had been arrested, but some things you just cannot keep to yourself. My relatives in England and Zimbabwe sent words of support and courage.

Ted had really found a way to make not only me suffer but each and every individual who had an ounce of care for me.

THIRTY-TWO
Hard Lessons Learned

One day, by chance, I called Norma's house when the police were still there. Nyasha put the lady officer on the phone. The cop informed me that Ted had indeed gained temporary custody of our kids and they were there to help him collect them. My sister had hid the kids in the basement until the police forced themselves in through a back door, setting off the alarm.

This was the day my nightmare truly began. For once he took the children from my mother's house, I would have no way of reaching them and talking to them. There would be no way of pretending that all was fine and that I would be seeing them soon. With his temporary custody order, the judge had also allowed him entry back into our home as long as I was incarcerated.

The day after he took the kids, Norma went to the house to check on the children, get my mail, as I was expecting a check from work, and to get my car, to which she had keys. Ted had come to the door with a towel around his waist. Over the phone, she would tell me their conversation.

He threatened, "You'll see Ruth when you all get deported. I'll make sure you all get deported. I am taking my kids and moving, and you will never see them again. Ruth doesn't own anything anymore. Ruth is on her way back to Africa. Everything that was hers is mine, and there is not a damn thing you can do about it, you fuckin' bitch! You can't do anything. Not a damn thing! You'll see her soon enough in Africa. You hear me? You're all going back, you fuckin' Africans."

In total shock, Norma had called the police to get any kind of help. The officers were polite, but regrettably they informed her there was nothing they could do about his refusal to allow her to see her grandchildren or his refusal to hand over my mail or my car. She explained to me how helpless and hopeless she felt after this altercation with him.

I had cried for her over the phone, feeling so guilty that I was putting my family in these circumstances. They were being humiliated by this asshole of a man, a man who had displayed that part of him in the very beginning. I, however, had been stupid and ignored the voice inside me that told me to run.

During this very week, one night as I slept, now clearly depressed, I began to think of something I had never allowed my mind to consider, something I had vowed I was too strong to succumb to.

I wrote this while in jail on January 13, 2009:

Feels like the end.

I closed my eyes to try to sleep last night and all I could see were images of my children's smiling faces. The tears started to flow from my eyes as if coming from a turbulent stream. I cried out, why me?

I have tried to be strong for 13 days, but last night was the weakest I've ever felt. For the first time in my life I wished I was no longer here in flesh, here to feel this pain, this anger, this hurt, this loneliness, this hopelessness, this misery, this agony, this curse, which seems to be stuck on me.

If I am His creation, then why do the worst things happen to me? I asked in silence. He gave me a mother, than took her away in the most tragic of ways. Well, some may argue those to be the wages of her sin, but what about my baby sister? He took her at the age of 3. What sin could she have possibly committed? Why did she have to die?

I survived through it all, and when I brought my own into this world, I was thankful and grateful. Now it's been 14 days without my heart's desire and my Handsome Boy. If I have sinned, then why should my children suffer?

I know not what awaits me tomorrow, but I know today feels like the end.

I had certainly become more spiritual, kneeling and praying in the middle of the night, right after the guards made their rounds. On this night, I was lying on my bunk. My eyes were swollen shut from the sheer volume of tears, burning hot from being rubbed so much and hurting from lack of sleep. I had what felt like an out-of-body experience. I saw myself get out of bed, holding one of my thin brown sheets in my hand. I saw myself twisting the sheet and tying it to one of the steel bars that separated the top part of the mod, on which the bunks were located, to the lower part of the mod, on which the dining and TV area were located. I saw myself take the other end and make a noose with it. I saw myself climb on the railing and jump off.

Once I realized what I was thinking, I felt as if a spear, reddened by coal, had been purposefully pierced through my heart. I cried with thoughts of the little girl in me, remembering how I had wished so much that my own mother had just held on for another day. I recalled how I would play over and over in my mind what would have happened if she had not turned into the train station that fateful day in 1985; how if only she had loved us enough, she would have conquered any sadness, any problem, and any situation.

Now I was lying here, thinking of taking my own life. If I could just find a little strength, it wouldn't matter even if I was deported back to Zimbabwe. Being the citizens they were, my children would grow up and look for me, wouldn't they? The pain of growing up without the person who gave birth to you, how would they live through it? I had done it, but it had not been easy. There was no way that I would give up on life that easily; no way I would allow him to win that easily. If there was anything in my power, I would pursue it in order to be reunited with my children one day, even if it took a lifetime.

Those who are ignorant about the plight of illegal immigrants in this country believe that most illegal immigrants have children here as a way to anchor themselves. I know that I planned and wanted to have my children because I really felt a maternal desire to have them. I really felt like I was ready to be a mother. Even with everything else that wasn't right in my life, my decision to have them was completely out of love and stemmed from nothing sinister.

The thing to remember is, illegal immigrants happen to be human beings, too. We have all the wants and desires that people who are not illegal have. Not having legal paperwork to reside in a country does not take away from our humanity.

We hurt. We laugh. We are also in constant "pursuit of happyness," just like everyone else.

That day, with my calling card, I dialed Ted's cell phone number. After the recorded warning by the message, informing him he was receiving a call from an inmate, he answered.

"What do you want?"

"I just need to tell my kids I love them."

"Well, now you know how it feels, don't you? I went two whole months without seeing them—"

I cut him off by saying, "Look, you won. You got me here. All I'm asking is to tell Chido and Simba that I love them. I don't have much time."

He hesitated, than called out their names.

Chido came on the phone. "Mom, are you in jail because you broke the law?"

"Yes, honey, I am in jail, but listen to me, okay? I want you to know that I love you so much, and I'll always love you, even if you don't see me for a really long time, okay?"

I couldn't push back the tears. After saying she loved me, too, she worriedly gave Simba the phone.

"Are you in jail, Mommy, cuz you're a bad person?"

"Handsome Boy, I need you to know that Mommy loves you so much, and that I'll always love you for as long as I live, okay?"

"But why are you sad, Mommy? Why are you crying?"

"I am crying because I miss you so much, and I wish I could hug you and kiss you."

"I love you, Mommy."

"I lov—" Before I could finish, someone hung up the phone.

I was relieved that they both sounded okay. They sounded healthy. However, I was perturbed that he had actually told them the truth about where I was. Norma had avoided telling the children, hoping I would soon be released, and they would never know what had happened to me. Their own father, for whatever his reasons may be, had told them. I was indeed in jail and not coming back to them.

Being arrested on New Year's Eve was hard enough, so was going into the New Year without my freedom. January 17 was now approaching. I had spent eighteen days behind bars, and celebrating my birthday behind bars was ponderous. There had been some hope I would be getting out, but then I found out that I no longer had a bond at all and was just being held in custody.

Norma had invited people over to celebrate my birthday and my eventual return home. They had sung for me in my absence and had cake in honor of my birthday. It was a nice thing for friends and family to do. Still, I felt as if I were dead now to the world, with things being celebrated in my honor and my memory.

A few days after my twenty-ninth birthday, this is the letter I wrote to Chrissy, with whom I would have been in Florida, celebrating my birthday on vacation like we had planned, if I was not illegal. The vacation had been booked and flight tickets bought. Instead, I was sitting in jail, writing this letter:

01-21-09

Dear Chrissy,

    I don't know where to begin. I guess I can start by saying I love you. I was up all night, last night, thinking about everything. Not knowing what will happen with me is really killing me and I somehow have this tremendous guilt that I'm stopping you from living your life. I feel as if you're going through everything I'm going through, and I hate that because I know just how painful it feels. I wish I could tell you that I'm coming home next week, but I don't know that. You may not see me for a long time. You may not see me at all. I want you to prepare for that. I may be forced to leave everything behind and start afresh somewhere else. That means leaving my kids, leaving you, leaving my family, my friends, my job, my house, my car, just so I can try to live a normal life again. I need to know that you will be okay if it comes to that. I will of course always stay in touch with you, no matter where I end up.

    This is the saddest letter I've ever had to write, but I have to. I need you to make yourself strong. I am so proud of you for all you're doing, going to school and working hard. You need to keep doing that. I know you're the one, and if that's how it was meant to be, then time and distance should not mean a thing at all. But if at any time you can no longer cope, then let me know. I love you enough to set you free. I just will always need you in my life somehow. I can never forget you. I am really looking forward to pictures of you.

    How I wish I could hold you in my arms again, wipe the tears from your face, tell you that I love you with all my heart and all my soul. I love you and I need you to know that. Write me back and let me know how you really feel about me, about us, about everything that's going on. Your support means everything to me. Your love is why I even get to smile. I spoke to your mom yesterday and she told me she loved me. I cried afterwards. I'm so humbled by the love your family has shown me. My *mom also told me she loved me, face-to-face, for the first time last week when she came to visit me. Isn't that something?*

I feel like I have known you a lifetime. I know I want to know you for the rest of my life. I don't want you to put your life on hold for me unless it's what you desire to do. I know we said it wouldn't be easy, but it's hard to believe it had to be this difficult.

I love you, baby . . .

After unreturned calls to wish me a happy birthday, my friend Carol had gone by my house to check on me. She arrived to see Ted in the middle of loading a U-Haul truck with furniture from the house. He had been rude and ordered her to leave. She had begged to know where I was. He told her that I was on my way to Africa, as he was getting me deported. Then he also told her about all the other supporting evidence he had presented to immigration upon returning into the home. He sifted through anything and everything, including essays I may have written in school or copies of documents.

It was because of the submission of these things that my bond had been scrapped and I now faced impending removal. I had signed to go before the judge within ten days, but that never occurred. Finally after nearly three weeks, my lawyer had a court date for me, January 29. With the new information, Carol had hunted Norma's number down, called her, and met with her at her house. She told her about what was happening at my old residence and also told her about all the things Ted had said to her. Now things made a little bit of sense, for Ted had indeed sealed my fate.

There would be no way I could walk the grounds of this country free again.

During the past twenty-eight days, I had filled my days with early-morning prayers, having received encouragement from the two ladies who conducted weekly Bible study at the jail, Kathy and Connie. I cried a lot and often, sometimes for hours. One day, I missed my kids so much I could not stop crying. After about two hours, the female guards had threatened to isolate me. They were afraid I was too depressed and might be suicidal.

"I just miss my kids. I'm sorry. I'll stop, but I just miss my kids." I released the sorrow.

I wrote letters to many people, mostly to Chrissy, whom I wrote every day, but I also wrote Ted's mother, telling her my thoughts, including the fact that her son had confessed he was gay. I told her the truth about how she had failed her son as a mother and had aided in his angry behavior, always finding fault in the women he was with and never with him. I must have written her ten pages or so. I remembered her home address, like I remembered many telephone numbers out of the blue. I guess desperate situations called for desperate measures.

I even wrote Ted a letter, one I would not send but kept as a way of getting rid of the anger I had toward him. If I was to ever succeed in whatever my future held, I knew I had to forgive him inside myself. So I put all my thoughts about him into this letter, which I kept in my green plastic container that held all my worldly possessions.

As January 29 approached, my stay here could not be described as "uneventful." No matter how much I kept myself busy with writing, including the first fifty pages of my life story, I found myself being picked on. One day after I had tried to joke with the other black girl in the mod—a completely innocuous and really unremarkable comment—she had forcefully slammed me against the steel bunk, almost snapping my back in two. I had to be isolated and given ice packs to help with the pain. Her use of force was completely unwarranted. It reminded me that people can just snap for no reason behind these walls. It made me realize that I was not in a safe environment at all.

I had seen many women from Mexico and El Salvador come and go within days, always opting to be returned to their home countries. They never seemed too disturbed by it. In fact, they were happy on the days they suspected they would be on a flight back home the following day. I envied them for this. If only my life was not as complicated; if only this had not become home to me over the last almost-ten years; if only I were not a mother to two young and hopeful citizens of this country; if only I were not a lover, a sister, a cousin, a daughter, a niece, and an aunt to people who lived here now. If only, maybe then I, too, would have checked the box to be returned to my country of birth.

Only, I knew I would not be happy. I knew too well the status quo of my birth nation: the cholera epidemic, the continuing political violence, the worst galloping inflation the world had ever seen. In simple terms, it was easily one of the worst places on the planet at this given time.

I entered the world in Zimbabwe, but I was choosing to continue my time on this earth in America. I had to fight and struggle and pray that this choice would be allowed.

I was called out very early the day of my appearance in court. On the drive to the Immigration Headquarters in Omaha, I sat unchained in the front seat, for everyone else going to court was male—a Sudanese guy and a few Hispanic fellows. The driver wanted to know each person's story. He was of Hispanic descent and had a kind tone in his voice, the total opposite of the red-haired ICE agent who had come to my home. (I will never forget that redheaded civil servant. He reminded me so much of Ted in his arrogance and lack of empathy.)

At the headquarters, I was once again placed in the now-familiar cold rooms, with the TV channel forever set on the Spanish show. I waited for hours for my turn to go before the judge. My size-small orange jailhouse uniform was now overly baggy and my pants were falling at the waist—evidence of the twenty pounds I had lost since the beginning of the month.

A young African-American female agent came to get me. I could not help but feel good that she was doing something productive and different from the many girls who failed to realize their potential in this country. She politely walked me into the courtroom, which was full. I took a seat next to my lawyer, Mr. Pheiffer, whom I was also meeting for the first time. I had spoken to him several times on the phone during the course of my incarceration. Across the room on the TV screen was Judge Fujimoto, a man of Asian descent, who presided as the judge for my hearing. That was another pleasant surprise. Seeing these faces of other races made me feel like I was not sitting in a room full of red-haired ICE agents.

In the time since I had been locked up, I kept thinking that had I been a white woman, with the same situation, or had my estranged husband been a black man, would I have been given such a steep bond and would things have gone the way that they did? Somewhere in my unconscious mind, the answer was no. Somewhere it always came back as things would have been much different had I been "privileged" enough to be white.

I had no doubt in my mind that my race played a factor with the decision ICE made to arrest me the way they did. I really believe that had my husband been black, like I was, they would have investigated further and would have discovered that his reporting of me was a direct result of him facing assault and domestic abuse charges. They would have come to the conclusion that it was in retaliation to my wanting a divorce.

ICE does not make a habit of arresting illegal immigrants who have not committed a crime—not counting their act of entering the country without proper documents—and are simply residing in their homes, doing nothing. Illegal immigrants are typically apprehended if they have committed a criminal offense beyond their lack of citizenship. I was sleeping in my own house when the agents came to arrest me. I can't think of any other reason for this besides the fact that I was an African black woman and the person who reported me was an American white man.

My lawyer began pleading my case to the judge, first telling him about my estranged husband, about my abuse at his hands, and about how he had taken everything, including my children. He demanded to know why bond had been revoked or set so high to begin with, even with the new evidence provided by Ted (the documents that he had found in the house after he had me arrested). My attorney concluded by saying I did not deserve to sit in jail and asked the judge for a low bail amount. The judge responded by granting bail set at $4,000. A glimpse of hope, finally.

When I returned to the cold room, two Hispanic girls were now in there. One had set her paper close to where I sat. Curious about her case, I picked it up and read it, asking if she didn't mind. This girl had come across the border and had no documents whatsoever; she had been arrested for driving without a license; her initial bail was set at $5,000 and had been reduced to $3,500. Now she was going back to court to see if it could be reduced further.

So illegal immigrants who came across the border were not punished as harsh as people like me, who had permission to enter, had passports and visas, who had then overstayed. I found this to be astounding. I had learned so many harsh realities of immigration since being arrested.

An Asian woman was in the mod now. She had arrived in this country as a one-year-old with her refugee parents from Laos. She had been a permanent resident with a green card for over thirty-five years; but after being arrested too many times for crimes like drug possession and prostitution, she was now facing deportation after serving her sentence for the crime.

Not having any family support or money to hire a lawyer, she spent a long time on immigration hold as she was trying to fight her case entirely on her own.

How would this even be possible?

Thousands of people leave their home countries every day in search of better lives and better futures elsewhere. My warning to all of you is be prepared, try as hard as possible to have a plan that actually works. Never leave your home country with the intent of staying as an illegal alien anywhere.

Of course, for one to come to that point, it's because all else has failed. I can honestly say from experience that being treated like a criminal and put behind bars for a long period of time is absolutely painful. The reality is some immigrants stay even for years behind bars because their countries don't want them. The immigration division misplaces their paperwork or they are trying to fight to stay without the help of an attorney.

As soon as any immigrant arrives in any new country, their first priority has to be their immigration paperwork. I wish I had known this. I wish I had been older when I arrived here. I wish I had had some guidance. I wish for so many things to have been different, but they were not. I simply had to deal with my situation the way it was.

By writing this book, I hope it opens up honest dialogue about people like me. I hope it puts a face to those of us who are or have been illegal—those of us who are minorities in any way, shape, or form. It gives some humanity to those of us cast with unfavorable labels.

Since leaving jail, I have read about other cases: some in which immigrants have died in custody, some have been sexually abused with absolutely no consequences for the perpetrators of these crimes. Many illegal immigrants in this country are treated with seemingly no human rights whatsoever. In such a great nation, where even those accused of terror are given some rights—like the right to be free of torture—then should people like me be treated without dignity or respect?

I am happy and proud that Chido, Simba, and Andre were born Americans and that no man or woman could ever put them in the place where I was put because they were not citizens. I am happy and proud that they will always have such great opportunities, if they take advantage of them. I hope that they will grow up to be proud Americans and will never need to seek a better life elsewhere. More than anything else, I pray that my children will grow up to be citizens who have concern for other people who may be different from them, that they would have hearts that accommodate all people from all walks of life.

THIRTY-THREE
Freed, But Am I Free?

Bail couldn't be processed that same day. On the following day after waiting anxiously all morning at midday, I was told to roll up. It was heartwarming to put on my own clothes again, my own underwear, even though all my clothes now had a slight funk from sitting in a container for a month. My jeans needed to be folded at the waist so they would not fall down. First it was Norma who was coming to collect me; then it was an ICE agent. It would be three more hours before he showed up. There was more waiting on the concrete benches in the cold rooms back at headquarters. Through the mirrored walls, the red-haired agent had seen me, and I heard him asking if I was being released.

I guess to people who do this kind of work, people like me have lives with no value and no purpose. The futures of the children we leave behind are not of concern to them. As much as people in health care are educated on the need for empathy, these people must be taught just the opposite: Never show compassion. Never show kindness. After all, you're only dealing with illegal aliens.

I was then called into the interrogation room and informed that I was going to have a GPS monitoring device placed on my ankle. I had to sign forms agreeing to charge it a minimum of two hours a day, as well as call to inform ICE if I planned a journey more than an hour out of town. I could shower with the device, but I could not submerge it in water. It took a while for the two agents to get it secured on my left leg; my small size was unfamiliar to them. After close to thirty minutes of trying, they finally had it secured. Initially it was as if I had a ball and a chain, but being freed made that seem like nothing. After the thirty days I had gone through, nothing could really faze me. If I had not died in that time, then this heavy thing around my ankle would not kill me.

The lady gave me back my driver's license. I asked twice, to make sure, if I still had privileges to it, and I was told yes. It was close to the end of the day and the place was empty. I was led to the waiting area where Norma had been stuck in for most of the day. I hugged her so tight. As we walked out, she began to cry, unable to understand why it had taken so long, why I had been the very last person to be released. She had seen many families get their loved ones and leave.

I think she cried mostly because, just like me, these past thirty days had been the worst days of her life. She explained how with death, at least the pain was final, you mourned and moved on; but with me behind bars, it had been a continual, endless mourning. I think she also felt overly guilty for the way I had come to this country, alone and unprepared. I think she blamed herself for all I had experienced, but I was out now and the worst of it was over.

In the car, my iPhone was still working. I sent a text out to Chrissy, saying, *I hope to see you later.* As if by fate, my cousin Timothy had arrived that very day from Canada to collect his wife and kids after gaining permanent residency in Canada. His place was our first stop. People were overjoyed, but they did not know what to say. I was hugged in as many ways as there are to be hugged. Some made light of the situation with humor and offering to fatten me up in no time. It had been weeks since the last time I heard from my children.

When you're in jail, weeks seem like months. I excused myself, went outside, and placed a call to Ted. He answered, and when I asked to speak to Chido and Simba, he said something about me giving him a chance to say something nice to me.

After everything that had transpired, he had the audacity to tell me that I should give him a chance to say something nice? Like what? What nice thing could someone who has taken you to hell and back have to say to you?

For as long as I might live, I will have no interest in anything that comes out of this man's mouth.

I spoke to my kids and told them of how I was hoping to see them soon. Back at Norma's house, Tashinga cried when she saw me. She had taken everything so hard, and it was so good to see Andre, as well as everyone else. I had a gazillion missed calls and messages on my phone. I just wanted a home-cooked meal and some rest.

Later in the day, Chrissy came over and demanded to know what I wasn't telling her. I still couldn't bring myself to be truly honest about my circumstances. I just wanted to be back and not answer questions. She respected that.

We drove to my house and I could not believe the shape in which Ted had left the place. He had taken almost all the furniture. He had left the kitchen table and microwave behind, as well as the computer desk and display cabinet. In the main bedroom, he had left some of my belongings in the closet and on the floor. But almost immediately I noticed that anything of value he had taken, like my Nike tennis shoes and my leather coats. The entire house was completely trashed. There was junk everywhere.

On the third day after my release, I had a meeting with a divorce lawyer working in the same office as Mr. Pheiffer. We discussed how I could get to see my kids again. While cleaning my house up, Norma had asked me to return to her house, for Ted had promised to bring the kids by for a couple of hours so they could see me. He had insisted I be at my mom's house when he dropped them off. Baffled, but glad at his act of kindness, I dropped everything and hurried back to Papillion.

Sure enough, he brought the kids. Like deja vu, my kids got out of the car and ran toward me, arms outstretched, calling out, "Mommy! Mommy!" This was my happiest moment of the brand-new year. They asked me many questions, and didn't know how to act. They clung to me as if their gogo, cousin, and aunts were strangers to them.

Simba had a lot of new words and facial expressions. He no longer talked like a baby, and Chido looked like she had grown a foot in the month I had not seen her. They were well groomed. Simba's long hair was in twists and Chido's was nicely done as well. Clearly, the touch of a female. "Latisha" was the name Simba uttered when questioned about who had done his hair. I had heard this name before; at this time, I was glad that whoever she was she seemed to have taken the time to make sure my children looked neat.

After two hours, he was back to collect them. It was sad having to say good-bye so soon, but I had nothing in writing that allowed me to keep them. They protested, especially my Honey Girl, who questioned why she couldn't stay. He hurried them off without offering her an explanation.

When I returned to cleaning my house, I noticed what had motivated Ted to make the act of kindness by bringing the kids. The microwave and the dishes that had been present in the kitchen, just two hours prior, were now missing. Knowing that once I was back, with the protection order that barred and removed him from the property regardless of ownership, he had found a way to lure me out of the house. This way, he could get the microwave. Now it was apparent that he had not finished removing everything he wanted to take from the property. Maybe initially he had taken his sweet time, confident that I would not return.

I would take seeing my kids again, even for a second, in place of a microwave any day. Anything material no longer held meaning in my life. I had lost my jobs on the very day of my arrest because the agents had sent faxes to my workplaces while I was at the headquarters. Ted had taken all the property; he had taken my car, which he refused to give back even after I begged for him to return it. He had taken my kids, too, and I had no idea where he had taken them.

My neighbors from across the street had come by to hear what had happened to me. They filled me in on all the details of what took place at the home when I was away. They had feared something terrible had happened to me. They knew of the attack; so when they noticed him returning to the home, they had watched his every move. He had indeed lived with a woman during the time he was at the house; and then he had been living not too far away, they suspected, as he was not gone too long with each load. A few guys had helped him move.

    I investigated further about the card left at my door indicating I was being subpoenaed. I met with Sarpy County prosecutors within the week. Now knowing that I had returned and had not been deported, like Ted and his lawyer had told them, prosecutors asked for the trial date of his assault case to be pushed back further to allow them time to question me and have me testify in the case.

    Ted was going to be tried for third-degree domestic assault and disturbing the peace. After sitting down with Mark, one of the prosecutors in the assault case against Ted, and explaining how Ted had attacked me the night of November 9, he was sure that felony strangulation charges should be added to Ted's charges, as he had clearly strangled me during the attack. The officer who took the initial report had missed this point somehow, hence the lesser charges.

    My cousin Octavia had come to visit me all the way from Long Beach; she was to return to the United Kingdom in the following months and had come to show her support for me. She sat through the meeting with me and had more questions for the prosecutors than I had. It was hard but freeing to reveal the truth about that night to the prosecutors in her presence. It was good to have her by my side, even just for a few days.

    I reported the incident with the microwave to La Vista police, and my neighbor had also informed me that Ted would often come to the house right after I left and let himself in. When I had rented a Dumpster, needing a way to clean the house out, he would come by and go through the Dumpster, sometimes even driving my car.

The mortgage had not been paid since I last paid it in December, and I had no money to pay for it now. I went to the hospital I had worked at and asked them for my last check, claiming the one they had mailed had been lost. They issued me a new one, so Ted had kept the other one but had not cashed it.

I also needed a copy of my W2, as that, too, was missing. With money from the check, I had to put some money down on the lawyer bills, which were staggeringly high. I tried to file for taxes through a Zimbabwean guy named Adam, who had his own office, but he could not process the transaction as it showed that someone else had already claimed my two children. Since I had tax return documents from day care showing I had spent close to $7,000 since July 2008 on day care, Adam advised me to take my completed forms by hand down to the Federal Revenue Building and to the Nebraska Revenue Building. While I sat in his office, Adam had surprised me by saying that he had heard I was dating women now. No point in denying it, I admitted it and we started a friendship of some sort.

My own friends seemed distant toward me. The first time I hung out with Brenna and Lucy, they managed to make fun of the whole situation. Lucy, a girl from Africa as well, had come here as a small girl with her family. She was well set with her green card and did not have the slightest idea about what I had been through. She even pointed blame on me for not having my things in order and therefore giving Ted the upper hand to achieve what he had.

I was so tired and did not even bother to explain the nature of my situation. I felt the sting of how people and friends change when things go wrong. I really could not blame them, for they could never know what it felt like unless they found themselves in the same situation.

THIRTY-FOUR
Discovering the Real Value of Life

Ted attempted to seem kind one more time, offering to leave the kids with me at Norma's for a few days. It was after Valentine's Day. Chido came, holding a balloon and a box that said *Happy Valentine's Day*. I smiled and thanked her, but I was livid that he would have the audacity to want to seem sweet. He gave me a garbage bag filled with some of my clothing.

With very little said to him, I drove my kids home to my aunt Norma's house, in her Dodge Nitro, which she would let me borrow on occasion. The other times, Chrissy was good at letting me use her car or taking me where I needed to go. After an hour of having the kids, I received a text from Ted saying that I needed to call him right away. He needed to know where his kids were. This moron was kidding, right? I called him on behalf of Chido and Simba.

However, after this happened over and over again, I became angry. He threatened to come and pick them up. I told him he could. As soon as I hung up, I called La Vista police. They had been trying to reach him to question him about the violation of the protection order.

Right when he pulled into the driveway, so did the police. He tried to negotiate with them, but they arrested him and took him to jail. I knew he wouldn't be in jail for more than a few days. It did not matter. I had my children with me; and for those few days, he had no say whatsoever. I had called around to my lawyers to see if anything could be done, but they did not think he would be there long enough for anything to be reversed.

In two days, an officer called, informing me of Ted's release and also asking if I would let him have the kids, since Ted had temporary custody. The officer insisted he could not make me give the children back to Ted, but he warned me that being in contempt of court could ruin my chances down the road. He assured me Ted would not come along, but instead his mother and his girlfriend, Latisha, would.

Latisha came to the door with the officer. She looked like she was sixteen, a little on the chubby side. Chido and Simba seemed comfortable around her. So, with tears in my eyes, I watched these people take my children away. Ted's stepfather had attempted to drive Ted's Infiniti parked on the street from the day he was arrested. I, however, had locked the steering wheel, asserting he could have it the moment he returned my car to me. His stepfather then went on to ask about the bag that was in the back of the car.

"Oh, you mean my hospital bag, which had all my mail in it? Sorry, you cannot have that" was my response.

It would take a fight and a long month for me to see my children again. My lawyer had proposed a temporary time-sharing arrangement and the return of my vehicle. Ted had turned around with demands of his own, including permission back into the home, to fix it up and rent it out. This person was beyond delusional. Even if I agreed to this, how do you rent out a house with three months of unpaid mortgage?

Ted also wanted some of the rest of his junk out of the garage and the shed. I had refused. I had stopped letting him win, and he was not going to get his way with me again, ever. So with every proposal, at the very last minute when he was to bring the kids to me, he would change his mind about something. My lawyer decided to remove everything else and leave the sharing of time. I would have the kids on Tuesdays till Fridays, and he would have them Fridays till Tuesdays. He turned down this temporary proposal.

The only thing my lawyer could do was take it to court. I had sat down with her and told her about his history, as I knew it: the number of children, the amount of past-due child support, the giving up of parental rights to one daughter, the emotional, verbal, and physical abuse. She made note of all these things and was prepared to go before the judge, but suddenly Ted buckled, agreeing now to sharing time and custody with me. I picked up the kids as soon as I could on that day.

So after almost four long months, I spent four days in a row with my kids, without any contact from Ted. Any contact from him would be a violation of the protection order. Per agreement, he was to be away from his residence in Onawa, which I had become familiar with in my search to get my car. An Onawa police officer had taken Chrissy and me right to the house to see if my car was there. The officer found it in Ted's locked garage, seen through a small window on the side of the building, and I had driven back to Omaha empty-handed. The Onawa police explained that their hands were tied, for they could not break into his garage. I would not be permitted to take my car, since I was still legally married to him. The officers were concerned that the car was still being considered marital property. It had been worthwhile, though. For on this day, I knew exactly where to go to pick up my kids.

I decided that all I could do was try to create new and happy memories for my children. Chido had missed me so much. She told me about how she prayed for me every night and how she saw me in her dreams when she slept. I told her I always dreamt of her and her brother as well. They both had become very fearful that I was leaving and not coming back. That very first week, they followed me everywhere, even the toilet. When I had to shower, they stood outside the bathroom door, crying for me not to go bye-bye and to let them in.

At night, in bed, they clung to me. My kids had suffered, just as I had in the time they had been separated from me. My kids were so different now. I don't know what happened to them since the time I was separated from them. I think over time the confusion about everything that was happening took its toll on them. They had both regressed in behavior, suffering from separation anxiety.

Simba started to exhibit very aggressive behavior, sometimes throwing himself on the ground in protest, or destroying things, especially his toys. Chido was now very sensitive and emotional. I had to take her to the doctor to get treated for diarrhea, due to the separation anxiety she had developed.

When I had explained to the doctor that I had been separated from my kids for about four months and really had no idea what had transpired with them during that time frame, the doctor was worried that Chido may have been subjected to some sort of sexual abuse. With that thought, the doctor conducted a full physical exam while I was in the room. She confirmed that everything looked as it should and that it mostly was due to emotional stress on a four-year-old. Chido was prescribed prebiotics for her gut to be put in her food. After a week, the diarrhea stopped.

Any attempt I made at disciplining Chido, even in the gentlest manner, would send her into a frenzy of tears. She cried to the point of vomiting when her dad returned to pick her up that first Friday. I had been talking to them all day, assuring them that I would be picking them up in a few days and promising that I would be there.

On the days I did not have my kids, I would spend the night at Chrissy's house, which was awkward, for she lived in her parents' basement. It was hard, but she had done so much for me. If these few nights with me in her parents' basement made her feel better, then I was willing to do it.

It was just really difficult. Her mom would have these days when she hated everything about the people we were: *gay*. She would quote Mormon Scripture and start heated arguments with us. We would question polygamy, which had been practiced in her faith. When she felt defeated, she threatened to kick Chrissy out. She wanted to know things about me that I did not think were any of her business. Finally, one day, we had a big argument. Chrissy's mom accused me of turning her daughter into the person she had become: "gay and liberal." She blamed me for all the problems in their family, blamed me for the way Chrissy felt so strongly about our relationship.

With this fight, I told Chrissy she had to move if she wanted me to be with her. I was not going to be insulted like that. I had spent thirty days in jail and was not taking it anymore. After being incarcerated, I realized something had changed within me. I was no longer willing to be a bystander to anyone or anything that insulted any part of my soul. I was just done with any part of myself being insulted. I had had enough. I would not take any more insults.

I was no longer going to be an outsider in my own existence. I would not stand to the side and watch my true self be compromised and denied.

The very next day, we had our own apartment.

After a long wait, my tax refund check came in the mail. I paid bills, lawyers, and planned a zoo trip with the kids the following Friday. Every Friday we did something special with the kids. The following Friday we all experienced IMAX 3D for the first time, watching *Deep Sea* at the Omaha Henry Doorly Zoo IMAX theater. We all went skating for the first time, and my two-year-old son had better skating skills than I. My daughter was just concerned with wanting the nice-looking white skates that another little girl was wearing. I promised her that once her skating skills were good enough, she could get a pair.

Before I went to jail, I thought I spent adequate time with my children. After being separated from them for so long, I realized that it was never enough. In our forced time apart, it occurred to me that I had worked incredibly long hours and had been in school for most of their toddler years. I had valued work more than quality time with my children. I just didn't know any better. Working hard was just something I had done since coming to this country at age nineteen.

I remember a time before I was married or had kids, and I had worked five straight twelve-hour shifts at the nursing home. When I was finally off for the weekend, I went to bed on Friday night and did not wake up till Sunday. An entire day had passed me by and I was not even aware of it. That really frightened me. I had worked myself into a mini-coma.

Unfortunately, this amount of binge working is a reality for most immigrants. Most of us are burdened with the obligation of sending money back home and helping our families that remain there. All we do is work, work, and work.

Now I spent my every waking moment immersed in my children's presence when I had them. I watched every little action they took; I listened to their every query. I hugged them and kissed them, telling them "I love you" at any moment of the day, not just when saying good-bye or when putting them to bed at night.

I had taken the blessing of having them for granted. I had taken my life for granted. Just the taste of fresh fruit or the act of spraying on perfume—when these simple, daily-life routines were withheld from you without your consent, these do become so vital, so significant.

When it was obvious that I was living with Chrissy, I sent an e-mail to Norma, my aunt who had grown to be my mom. It read in part:

I have so much to tell. I'm not even sure where to start. Some of the things are things that I have buried so deep down.

Firstly I love you so much and I am so blessed and lucky to have you. For the longest time I was too angry at my biological mother for taking her own life and not loving me and my sister enough to rise above it, but I've gone through school and really learned the effects of mental illness. For every person who commits suicide, they're mentally sick and without help cannot help what they do. I've since forgiven her, and having Chido and Simba closed the void I always felt. There was a time I was mad at the whole world, a time I didn't believe I would be alive this long. I now know that I have a purpose and that I wasn't a mistake and that, no matter what, God loves me.

So I'm sure by now you have realized that I am gay. I'm sure you wonder how this all came about. The truth is, when I was in high school, I found myself really attracted to certain female teachers and certain older girls. At the time I just thought I admired them for their beauty and intelligence, but I knew it was more than that. I knew it was morally wrong to feel the way I did, so I liked guys like I was supposed to.

I have this image in my mind. I'm about 4 or 5 years old. I am living with Gogo in Murehwa. One day I was at a neighbor's house and a man from that house took me to the cornfield and tried to rape me. I was too small to fight him off. He tried to force himself on me, but he failed. He got me up, cleaned the dirt on my clothes, and took me back. I've never told a soul about this, but it happened. When I've been in relationships with men, it was fine. The problem came when they wanted to be intimate with me. I was never comfortable, and I always felt violated.

I've done some research about gayness. According to research, 90% of gay people like me are just born that way, but there was also a strong correlation with sexual abuse from the opposite sex as a child, and also lack of a bond and attachment to the parent of the same sex also contributed to why some people are gay. For me, it could be any or all of these. I've just come to terms with it. I've prayed about it; I've been sad about it, but now I just embrace it.

I just hope that you will accept me the way I am and you won't think that I can change the way I am. I've tried to be with a man. I'm just not meant to be with one. I have no desire to be with one.

Being with a woman is just like any relationship. We don't always agree and nothing is guaranteed. I just want you to know that I won't be with a man ever again, because I really enjoy being with a woman. I never feel violated and I never have to worry about my children being violated. I don't trust men; I never have, and not being with one is like this heavy load being lifted off my shoulders.

God loves us all and Jesus died for our sins. I'm actually happy inside for the first time in such a long time. So far, most of my friends know and have been supportive. Timothy knows, Adam knows, and eventually people will know I'm not embarrassed by it. Life is short, and I just want to live my life as if tomorrow is my last day.

Stay blessed. When I do write my book, all these things will be revealed. I wanted you to hear it from me.

I love and appreciate you.

Love always,
Your Daughter

I got absolutely no response from Norma, the woman who was more than an aunt, the woman who was my mother. She acted as if she never received this e-mail from me. I know she did receive it. It wasn't trapped in a spam filter or lost in her cyber in-box. My cousin Nyasha mentioned that my aunt had said something about the e-mail to her. Also, during a minor argument I had with my aunt, she stated that she couldn't believe I was trying to blame my "gayness" on the fact that my mother was absent in my life. This was something I had only alluded to in the e-mail.

It was very clear to me that she had no interest in discussing the issue with me. Even more than that, my aunt seemed offended by the e-mail altogether. Her attitude toward me was rather callous after I sent the letter.

THIRTY-FIVE
A Day of Reckoning Arrives

I met with the new prosecutor handling Ted's case, for it had now been moved to a district court. She explained the ways in which they could offer a plea bargain for him to plead guilty. She was from Australia, and meeting and seeing people who had originated from elsewhere made me realize that this country truly is made up of immigrants. She also mentioned they were looking into the issue with my car. I had filed an official stolen vehicle report under the "theft by unlawful taking" law.

It had taken a long time, but I was in the courtroom on the day he pleaded guilty to third-degree domestic assault/violence and to misdemeanor theft of a vehicle. The prosecution had dropped the charges of strangulation and violation of protection order and lessened the theft from a felony to a misdemeanor. Ted stood before the judge with tears running down his cheek as he admitted to the charges after initially trying to bring in the fact of my arrest, which the judge hailed as irrelevant to his charges. Ted faced a maximum of a year for each count. He was sentenced to one year in jail, which was automatically reduced to six months. He eventually was behind bars for four months in total, in the same jail that I had been in, the Cass County Jail. Maybe karma is a bitch, after all.

During this stressful time, when I had gone to Iowa to collect the kids after Ted's sentencing, his girlfriend, Latisha, tried to prevent me from taking them. She slammed the door, asking that we leave her porch. Chido ran out of the house and into my arms; Simba remained behind the closed door. I could hear her telling him to tell me that she was his mom and that I was being sent back to Africa.

When she opened that door again, she referred to me as "Africa," and called me every name in the book. The only thing that stopped her from hitting me was the Mace I held in my hand, ready to spray when provoked. So this was what it had come to: me fighting some girl for my court-ordered visit; her coming out of a house filled with things I had bought; them keeping the precious baby albums I had spent hours putting together, keeping all my children's portraits, some I had spent a lot of money on.

It wasn't the furniture I cared about, but the sentimental things. There were items I wanted my children always to remember me by—the things about their birth and infancy that only their mother could show. Ted's keeping of these things is what broke my heart. I couldn't help imagining this woman who hated me so much, who wished so much that I would just be deported so she could replace me in my children's lives, going through those precious baby books and reading the personal letters intended for Chido and Simba's eyes only. She could become jealous of the emotion I showed in these private letters and, out of spite, rip them apart and toss them away like garbage.

After this incident, I had managed to get my son, after all, and Ted's attorney withdrew his services of representing him. For the meantime, I had my children back.

I had no official job, but I was helping a friend during nights with an elderly couple, who needed someone else in the home. I had signed papers from Attorney General Jon Bruning accepting their decision to revoke my nursing license for two years, not sure what happened with it afterward. In my mind, I knew that even if I could never practice as a nurse another day in my life, the knowledge I gained through the process would always remain with me. The people I met—from classmates, teachers, coworkers, and, most important, patients whose lives I may have impacted—would always remain with me. Nothing could erase these experiences—not revocation or deportation.

With no way of paying the money owed on the house, I planned to file Chapter 7 bankruptcy as soon as I had the money needed to do so. I need to let go of the memories it held, especially my ties to Ted.

I spent my nights writing this story about my life in the hope that no matter what happens to me—whether I lose my immigration fight to remain here with my children, my family, and my friends, or if I am six feet under—Chido, Simba, Andre, Bobbi (a little girl my aunt Norma adopted), and now my new baby nephew, Roman, can grow up and read the truth about their mother and their aunt.

The children in my life can value the freedom they truly have of being born American and being born truly free.

THIRTY-SIX
Forgetting, Forgiving, and Forming a Future

After Ted was sentenced to six months in jail for assaulting me and stealing my vehicle, I was granted temporary full custody of my kids. In December 2010, my divorce was finalized and I was granted sole physical and legal custody of our children, but it didn't come easy. After Ted's release from jail, he focused his attention on proving that I was an unfit mother.

On one of his visits with the kids, he had taken Chido to the ER and reported that I had apparently smacked her across the face, leaving a scratch. Next thing I knew, within thirty minutes of him picking the kids up, a cop showed up at my door to investigate this alleged abuse. I was shocked but not surprised. Luckily, the Papillion Police Department was now familiar with my situation, and the cop explained to me that he would have to log the complaint with social services for them to further investigate.

Next thing, social services was knocking at my door a few weeks later. Apparently, since I was a lesbian, I had to be sexually abusing my daughter. They interviewed Chrissy and me and asked us questions such as "So what kind of affection do you show each other around the kids?"

To that, I responded, "We show each other the kind of affection I would show if I was with their dad or any other man, for that matter. We are in a relationship. We hold hands. We kiss and we cuddle around the children. It is what two people who are in a romantic relationship do with each other."

After also going to my children's school and interviewing the teachers there, the social workers concluded that Ted's allegations were "unfounded," but it wasn't the end. He kept going back to them with one claim after another, until they asked me to take my kids to Project Harmony, where professional counselors could interview my children in my absence and make a determination of what was really going on.

I could not believe that Ted was really now doing this to our children, forcing them to lie, emotionally abusing his own children just to make me suffer. During the interview, Chido disclosed how Ted had coached her to tell lies about me. She started crying, saying she knew that her mother loved her and that I had never done anything but care for them.

After this interview, I was informed that if Ted attempted to make any more false claims against me, he would be criminally charged. Every single claim he had made against me was unfounded, and my lawyer and I now had a stack of files to show the judge. These documents illustrated the length to which he was willing to go to make my life miserable and to show that he really did not have the best interest of the children at heart.

So in the end, all he tried to use against me in court was that I was illegal, being deported, and gay. However, the judge was more interested in the kind of parent I had been to my children. It is still an ongoing struggle. I have tried to forge some civil understanding with Ted for the kids' sake. But even on his visits, he and his girlfriend, who we discovered was only seventeen when he started dating her in 2008, still tell my children that I am being deported and that Latisha will be their mother. It's sad and heartbreaking.

After my own release from jail, I must admit that I went through a grief process. I was deeply angry at everything and everyone. While Chrissy really tried her best to be there for me and make everything okay, I took out a lot of my frustrations on her. She was ready to settle down and have a family. She was so devoted to the children and to me.

Meanwhile, I was coming out of a very abusive six-year marriage that was as ugly as it could get. She was the first woman I had been with; and after coming out, all of a sudden, a world of women found me desirable. I had no idea how to react to this sudden attention. It was everywhere.

When we were out having dinner, some woman would hand me her card or say how cute I was. I could be at the grocery store and women were smiling at me differently. Even women I had worked with, whom I had known to be straight all along, were confessing their attraction toward me. It was overwhelming and I was unprepared for it. Men had never shown me that much attention. It was insane.

In the end, Chrissy suffered a lot due to my immaturity in my newfound sexuality. After being cheated on more than once and finding out about it, after many breakups and getting back together, after close to three hard years together, Chrissy finally walked away from me for good. She didn't want to be friends or even have anything to do with the children. It was easier for her that way.

I have deep regrets about the mistakes I made with her, about the way I treated her in the end. I have done my best to apologize for the person I became to her. She has not wanted to hear my apologies and I totally understand. I reflect constantly and have taken steps to work through my own issues in therapy so that I will not treat anyone else the way I treated Chrissy.

One of the "gifts" that Chrissy gave me was her advice that I should see a therapist, a woman she had seen in the past. I followed her directive, and Susie was amazing. I had never before sought therapy for myself, but I was so grateful once I began. I would sit down for an hour at a time and just talk and talk and talk. Susie mostly just listened. It was something I needed, and it was something I should have done, probably since childhood. Being in therapy helped me tremendously.

I am still trying to learn from my own mistakes. I'm still growing. I have been with other women since, but meaningless relationships are just that—even when you finally discover your true identity. When my heart has been truly moved, something else got in the way. There is always a little karma in life.

After Chrissy left, I had to really learn to be a single mother. I had taken for granted so much of what she did. While it has been painful to let go of her and what we had when it was good, it has also given me a chance to truly stand on my own two feet, to truly throw myself into the role of mother. It allowed me to concentrate on my passions without worry, to figure out who I truly am.

My children have also reaped the benefits of therapy and are happy at home and in school. At age nine, Chido is more than excelling academically. She was selected into the "High Ability Learner" program last year in third grade. Kids who are selected into this gifted program have to have scored 96% or better on their NeSA (Nebraska State Accountability) test scores. She is so proficient in reading that she scored a 100% in the NeSA test. Chido loves art and music and science.

She has been in Girl Scouts since kindergarten and loves everything about it. She is polite and kind, and has grown so tall that she is up to my shoulders already. She is more beautiful than I ever was, but she is humble. I couldn't have been blessed with a better daughter.

My son, Simba, who struggled with behavior problems at the beginning of first grade, has now fully adjusted. He is proving to be just as smart as his sister. He is a car enthusiast, just like his father. He makes it a point to get a classic-car book from his school library almost every week. He is very athletically gifted and I am trying to get him signed up for a lot of different sports. Both my kids have taken swimming, gymnastics, and this year basketball lessons.

Simba wanted to be in Boy Scouts, but I could not allow him because of the organization's stance on those who are LGBTQ. I simply refuse to have my kids associated with any groups that allow discrimination. I know that may not be fair for my children to miss out on things because of my beliefs. However, I'm striving to bring up children who are not sheltered.

I want them to be children who can love and appreciate all people. I am trying my best to raise them as differently from the way I was raised as possible.

I call my kids "Honey Girl" and "Handsome Boy," because my daughter is the color of honey and my son is handsome. I also do it because as a child growing up, there was something reassuring about the fact that my grandmother had a nickname for me. No matter what was going on, I felt loved anytime my grandmother called me "Wheety girl." It made me feel special and loved; and I hope my kids feel the same way when I call them by their nicknames, which is almost all the time. They have already done so much for me in this life. I cry a lot on their birthdays or anytime they accomplish any little milestone that I never got to experience with my own mother. That deprivation is never far from my mind.

THIRTY-SEVEN
New Horizons and Different Directions

The elderly couple I was taking care of at night soon suffered worse and worse health scares. First the husband endured many illnesses and heart attacks. He grew more frail, was confined to a hospice, and passed away. His wife was just never the same after his death. She was in and out of the hospital, until her children decided it would be better if she stayed at home and received care there. They did not anticipate a long life awaiting her.

Being pragmatic, I knew I had to do something about finding another source of income. From the experience I had gained helping Chrissy and her mom with their cleaning business, and having worked those many years ago as a housecleaner in England, I decided I would try that. I would start my own cleaning company and work for myself. Online I found a kit that had lots of information and advice; I purchased it for about $19. It basically listed everything I would need in order to begin this business. It also advised on how best to advertise for such an enterprise.

While I was working nights, taking care of the elderly lady in her last days, I was trying to start this new business. I had been so fortunate to have the experience of taking care of this couple. Tucked away during my many nights with them reminded me of the time I had spent with my own grandmother, nestled away as an infant in our little hut in her village.

There is something truly healing about spending time with elderly people. They have a sense of wisdom that only comes with being alive for a long time. Even though it was work, it was good for my spirit. I appreciated the experience more than they could ever know.

I sat down with my pastor and told him about my plan to start a cleaning business. He offered all the extra cleaning tools he had in his own house. He gave me my first mop and bucket for my business. I also sat down with Carole Souza, a woman whose business sense I really respected. She gave me sound advice on what entailed running a good business.

Once I placed an ad on Craigslist, I got a call within the week and cleaned my very first house. By the time the elderly lady I was helping take care of passed away, my cleaning business was steadily growing. I hired an aunt of mine, who had come to Omaha in order to provide a DNA sample to be matched to her son. He had committed suicide.

My aunt's son had come here on a student visa. As far as we knew, he was in college and had a job at the time he took his own life. I know that I cannot judge him. I know all too well how overwhelming being young and alone in a foreign country can be. It can be utterly brutal; he just couldn't take it. My aunt's help in the business made a big difference. We could clean more houses in a day together than one person could. We both steadily started making a living this way.

Running my business, I've been touched and gratified by some of my clients, who are devout Conservative Republicans. They know the entirety of my story and see my humanity. Underneath it all, really, we are all people. That acceptance gives me hope.

Many of the people I have met in these past few years—greeting them as my authentic, true self—have shown me that I am not an outsider at all. I am just like everyone else. The thing about authenticity is that when people can love you as yourself, you can see the good in the world.

There really is a lot of good.

By chance, one night when I was at a friend's house on game night, someone had mentioned having a house for rent. I inquired about the house's location and it turned out to be right in my neighborhood, literally three minutes from my kids' school. My children and I had been living in a low-income-housing apartment since November 2009. We had briefly shared an apartment with Chrissy, but she had kicked me out after I cheated on her.

I found myself back at Norma's house with my two kids. There was no room for our clothes. I had to keep some of our wardrobe in my aunt's garage and some in a house she had bought with the hope of turning it into a group home. She had been working on that project for a year or so, but nothing fruitful ever came of it.

I had been lucky to get the low-income apartment because I was essentially self-employed. As such, I didn't have paycheck stubs for verification, but the authorities worked with me. I was ever so thankful.

In June 2012, my kids and I moved into the rental house. They finally could ride bikes around the neighborhood and have friends over. We have even celebrated their birthday parties in our own backyard—a dream that was important back during the purchase of my first house with Ted and never vanished.

THIRTY-EIGHT
On a Righteous Path for My Rights

Almost immediately after being released from immigration detention, I became an LGBTQ activist by accident. Within the first two weeks of being released from jail, I attended church with my aunt Norma. We went to Glad Tidings, and I was shocked to hear the pastor denounce a Lutheran board's decision to appoint a lesbian to head one of its churches. As soon as he stepped onto the pulpit, before he had even greeted his congregation, he had raised a newspaper and expressed his disgust that a church would allow a homosexual to hold such a position.

I felt my blood boiling while I sat in that church. If I hadn't been there with my aunt and my cousin, I would have gotten up and left. I heard nothing from the rest of his sermon because I was so angry.

How can church be a place where some people are turned away? How can some people think they have a right to remove God's love from anybody, to dictate who is loved by God and who is not? For the first time, I really felt the discrimination and challenges faced by people who are LGBTQ and I was floored.

My anger would not let me remain silent. After the service, I found myself walking right up to this man and telling him my story. Almost in tears, I told him I was a good person, a good mother, and that he had no right to say that I was not welcome in the eyes of God.

That was my very first act of activism. My second act was to find a new congregation and church.

Over the years, my newfound activism has taken me to all corners of this country. I traveled to Yale University in February 2013, where I presented my story as one of the featured speakers at the IvyQ conference, an annual conference for Ivy League LGBTQ students. It was an unforgettable experience. My stay in Connecticut was extended by the arrival of storm "Nemo," which dumped up to forty inches of snow in some parts of the northeastern United States. I had never seen that much snow in my life.

On this trip, I got to experience New York City for the first time. I was lucky to have my friend Greg, a lifelong New Yorker, take me to a lot of historic sites in the city. We had drinks at the Stonewall Inn in Greenwich Village, the site of the Stonewall riots of 1969. This skirmish is widely considered to be the single most important event leading to the gay liberation movement and the modern fight for gay and lesbian rights in the United States. He took me to the site of the Twin Towers, where new construction to replace those destroyed in the terrorist attacks in 2011 was under construction. New York City was very much like everything you see in the movies: lots of yellow cabs and NYPD police cars on the streets, lit billboards and tall, magnificent, historic buildings.

One of the things that has helped tremendously over the last few years has been my church community. They have been fully supportive about all the aspects of who I am. Within six months of being a member at Metropolitan Community Church (MCC) Omaha, I was elected to their board of directors. I went to Washington, D.C., for a "People of African Descent" conference, which is done every three years by MCC churches.

I fell in love with all the historic sites that city holds, its majesty and history. I stood in front of the Lincoln Memorial and the White House. It was the stuff dreams are made of. I went to St. Louis for another conference for MCC churches and had the privilege to stay at the historic Union Station Marriott hotel. I was fortunate to share this experience with Chrissy before our final breakup. We enjoyed downtown and toured the beautiful St. Louis Arch. I just wish we hadn't fought so much on this trip. Our once-beautiful romance was fast becoming ugly and falling apart.

When the horrific tornados hit Joplin, Missouri, our sister church there was completely destroyed. I was part of the group of volunteers from MCC Omaha who offered to go and help. That experience further changed my life. To see miles and miles of complete destruction and people coming together, still appearing hopeful, even when some of them had lost everything—simply put, it was inspiring.

I was reminded that all of us have storms to face and adversity to overcome.

THIRTY-NINE
The Battle Rages On

There have been days I have stayed in bed because I was too depressed to get out of it. There have been days I have cried rivers, not knowing how I was going to feed my kids or how I would pay rent, but I have managed. Doors have opened up for me—one way or another.

I've realized that African Americans still have battles to win. Even though it has been decades since the civil rights movement, stories like that of Trayvon Martin's are stark reminders that the fight for equality for African Americans is really not over yet in this country. Racial discrimination, though more discreet and exercised through means like racial profiling nowadays, is still very much alive in the United States.

It is a reality of life, but it doesn't have to be a fact of life. It can be changed. It must be changed. We all can work together to attain that goal.

I wish I could be writing about how my immigration fight is long over and I no longer worry about my fate. Unfortunately, after my VAWA approval, my green card application was denied. When I received the denial, I scrambled around for lawyers who could help. My lawyer who had helped me so far was in failing health and was no longer being effective. I found an immigration firm in town that really believed in my chances. We hurried and filed "cancelation" paperwork, only to hear back that immigration had not, in fact, filed the denial officially. They were still looking into the case.

So we are waiting to hear back.

I am still in limbo.

I still do not know what my fate will be.

What I do know is that after I went public with my story in January 2012, I have become somewhat of a public figure and have had numerous interviews with African and American media. I have faced numerous threats, especially from fellow Africans and Zimbabweans, for gay rights are still very much a taboo in most parts of that continent.

In my own country, its president, Robert Mugabe, has publicly denounced homosexuality and has compared people like me to pigs and dogs. It is not safe to be openly gay or lesbian or transgender where I come from. The conditions for people like me keep getting worse. There is a growing intolerance and rampant homophobia where I come from, as well as in other African countries.

In Uganda, they have recently proposed a bill to kill homosexuals. In Nigeria, Cameroon, and Zimbabwe, they are considering life imprisonment as punishment for homosexuality. In many parts of Africa, homosexuality is still illegal and a crime. This recent surge of intolerance is attributed to the popularity and increased fight for LGBTQ rights in Western nations, especially here in the United States.

I don't think my life would ever be safe in Zimbabwe or anywhere in Africa. I speak now because in those areas I'm speaking behind a keyboard and computer screen. I know that these people who threaten me cannot carry out their threats, since they cannot physically get to me. I do it because in my speaking and activism, I receive so many messages from people still there who are living in the shadows and in hiding. These folks are aware of their sexuality, but they are trapped in intolerant societies. They feel hopeless, and I speak for them. I have come to believe that those of us who have free rein should speak on the behalf of those who cannot. Otherwise, change will just never come.

I just try to share as much about my life as I can to try and change the minds and hearts of those who are intolerant and to give hope to those who have none. I hope I'll always have the free space to speak, not just about LGBTQ issues or immigration issues, but about injustice wherever they exist.

Five years ago, I didn't even know what activism was. Today, like Alice Walker once said, "Activism is the rent I pay for living on this planet."

EPILOGUE
My Heart and Courage Grow

I was single for almost three years, falling for all the wrong people, and nothing ever really working out. At some point, I discovered that sleeping around with women I had no emotional bond with was monotonous, so I stopped doing it. In the last year, I paid a visit to my OB-GYN and had a thorough workup of blood testing and STD testing done. It is a relief to know that I remain STD and disease free.

Looking in the news at how other countries and cultures have been subordinating their female populace, I know that I am very privileged to live in a place where as a woman I have access to health care.

Within this last month, I have found myself falling in love. She came out of nowhere, laced with an Australian accent, and boasting freckles on her face like stars in the night sky. She is eleven years older than I am. She is a mother, a writer, and a feminist, who knows her place of privilege as a white woman in this world.

I wasn't looking for love when Deanne showed up. Even though we live worlds apart, there is something about our endless conversations and the way she looks into me when we Skype that has me staying awake at night. There is something undeniable about her convictions that give me peace of mind. Because my immigration situation is still in limbo, I have felt like true love was just not in the cards for me, yet here we are.

To mark our first month of this utterly unexpected distant-love adventure, here is what she wrote to me: *You are gorgeous. Happy one month of conversation and held breath and sideways glances and gentle words and delighted discovery of a shared hungry sexuality. Happy one month of thinking and yet sometimes being too side-struck to think, of touching yet being too distant to touch, of synchronicity yet living in different days.*

OUTsider

I am reminded of my furtive reading of a self-help sex guide before I truly came out to myself and to the world. I tried to hide the title of the book I was reading on my trip to California. I was afraid of what the other airport travelers would say or think or feel about me.

Now I know that I am free to be who I always was. I have come out as an illegal immigrant, a lesbian, a onetime abused wife, a proud mother, and a tireless activist. I have spoken up about the things that used to weigh me down—the things that I fought so hard to keep secret.

Today I speak openly about them. Once I was an outsider and I was fearful. Now I am an outsider and it gives me strength and hope.

ACKNOWLEDGMENTS

I would like to thank my publisher, Scout Publishing LLC, for how honored I've felt through the process of digging deeper into my life story with your support. Publisher Ryan Sallans, editor Stephanie Finnegan, and art director Erika Block—I humbly want to thank each of you for your insight and dedication to this book, but mostly for seeing my humanity and believing in my story.

I would also sincerely like to thank the team at Curley Immigration Law PC LLO, especially Mark Curley and Pamela Bloch, for taking on my case with humility and for being willing to fight for my cause while ensuring that I continue to live my life fully. Words cannot express my gratitude.

Pascal, a friend from nursing school, has become my best friend in every sense of the word. In the times I have been most desperate, he has been there to offer an ear when I need someone to listen, or even money when he could tell I could use it. Pascal and his wife, Essi, are some of the best human beings I have ever met in my life. Our kids are best friends and I'm so thankful for his unwavering friendship and encouragement.

I've met incredible people, like Erin Anderson, who has become a dear friend because of her passion for activism and whose parents died in a murder-suicide a few years ago. We are both mothers, and both gay women. We have both lost parents in horrific, tragic ways. I think our similar struggles cemented our friendship.

My path has crossed with women like Felicia Webster and Michelle Troxclair, who created "Verbal Gumbo," a popular poetry night in the city of Omaha. They are two African-American women who are passionate about education and literature. They have given me a completely different view on African Americans as a whole. Through their friendship, I've gained better knowledge and understanding of what it means to be an African American in this country.

OUTsider

I have met people like Delaney Kiernan, a young kid from Gowanda, New York, who is in the U.S. Air Force. She is like my platonic wife, since we are pretty much the same person. She just happens to be white, from a small town in New York, and speaks with a heavy New York City accent. I happen to be black, from a small village in Zimbabwe, and speak with an accent that is all over the place.

Melissa Magano Kandido is a passionate teacher who is married to a Namibian man. She has invited me to speak to her middle-school students at the school where she teaches. I've met clients in my business, like Tim and Kim, and countless others who exemplify humanity and who don't see me any differently.

To my wonderful children, Chidochemoyo and Simbarashe, your unconditional love for me gives me wings. It is my prayer that you will both always have the courage to be authentically yourselves; my love for you is never ending.

To my family at large, all my cousins, aunts and uncles, you have really been my mothers, fathers, sisters, and brothers. I wouldn't have made it this far in life without you.

To all family and friends whose support and love for me has never wavered: Octavia and Ivan, Aunty Algar, Allen and Thandie, Grace, Barbara and Jeremy, Memory, Trudy, Lucy, Brenna, Jenny and Ed, A'lice and Larry, Jackie, Gabi and Jenn, Heather Wilhelm, Pasi, Carole Souza, Kevin Merik, Annett Billings, Tom Emmett, Mary and Cheryl, Keith and Jessie, Gerard, Michelle, Melissa Smithee, my entire CLM class at MCC, the entire Zimbabwean community in Omaha, and all those I have not named, I thank you deeply.

To Chrissy, for giving me the courage to stand at a time when it seemed impossible. I will always cherish you.

To my nephews and nieces, Bobbi, Andre, Roman and all the ones I am yet to meet, Thalia and Marisa and the ones back in Zimbabwe and the United Kingdom, please know I will always be there for you.

To all the loved ones I have lost since my departure from Zimbabwe—my grandmother Milka Murehwa, my aunt Lucy, my aunt Emma, my uncle John, my cousins Lydia, Tawanda, and Tafirenyika, and the ones not mentioned—I am so sorry that I won't get a chance to see you again in this life. Thank you for loving me.

To the relatives who have never had a chance to know me because of distance, I will make an effort to know you better.

To my mother, my aunt Norma, thank you for bringing me so far. I know it hasn't been easy, but we have the rest of our lives to figure it all out. I love you.

Metropolitan Community Church of Omaha and every single person I have met there, thank you for taking me in, just as I am.

To my birth mother, Norah, I am a spitting image of you, and I wouldn't want it any other way. Thank you for bringing me into this world.

My baby sister, Chido, I only wish I had a little more time with you. I hope I make you proud.

To the new person in my love life, Deanne, as much as I try to put into words what having you in my life is like, words still fail me. You are beautiful, passionate, and so adored. The thought of a shared life with you brings me endless smiles.

For my grandmother, my birth mother, and my baby sister, by telling my story, I am also telling all of yours. Your legacy lives on. RIP.

SUGGESTED READING

Here is an informal listing of some books that helped me in my understanding of myself and of the world around me:

The New Jim Crow: Mass Incarceration in the Age of Colorblindness by Michelle Alexander

The Other Side Of Paradise – A Memoir by Staceyann Chin

Adam's Gift: A Memoir of a Pastor's Calling to Defy the Church's Persecution of Lesbians and Gays by Jimmy Creech

Same Sex in the City (So Your Prince Charming Is Really a Cinderella) by Lauren Levin and Lauren Blitzer

Second Son: Transitioning Toward My Destiny, Love and Life by Ryan Sallans

Black, White & Jewish: Autobiography of a Shifting Self by Rebecca Walker

Like Me: Confessions of a Heartland Country Singer by Chely Wright

ABOUT THE AUTHOR

Ruth Marimo was born and raised in the Southern African country of Zimbabwe. In 1999, at the age of nineteen, after arriving in England she found herself booking a round-trip ticket to the United States. She never boarded her return flight. Ruth now lives in Omaha, Nebraska, where she feels her number one job is raising her two beautiful children. To support her family, she owns a small residential and commercial cleaning business, and in her free time she continues to work on her writing, advocating for immigration reform, and speaking out against the mistreatment of LGBTQ people in Africa. You can learn more about Ruth's current work by visiting her website: ruthmarimo.com.

www.ingramcontent.com/pod-product-compliance
Lightning Source LLC
Chambersburg PA
CBHW051423290426
44109CB00016B/1405